"The things which are impossible with men are possible with God."

(Luke 18:27; KJV)

1

iT ALL STARTS WiTH ONE STEP

WRITTEN BY:

BRADY SiLVERWOOD

Printed in United States of America.

ISBN: | 9798884473195 (hardcover) |
ISBN: | 9798884964563 (paperback)|

Cover design by Kyle Aitken.
Edited by Danyel Meahan.
For more author information, visit
https://www.bradysilverwood.com

Scan to visit Brady's Website!

Dedication

I would like to dedicate this book to Liam Hearne. Liam was born with cystic fibrosis, a rare life threatening disease that damages the lungs and digestive system. Doctors didn't think Liam would live past two years. Liam ended up living for twenty-four years and graced everyone who met him with all of his light and faith. Thank you for showing me how to live my life to the fullest, Liam. I will honor you with every breath!

Liam Hearne 09/20/1991 - 12/16/2015

Contents

Foreword by Luke Gledhill

I am blessed and grateful for the opportunity to write this foreword about an incredible and inspiring human being. In my eyes this is not a self-help book, this is a real story about how anything is POSSIBLE. Even when you think the odds are stacked against you, you can keep moving one step at a time. Reading this book will give you the opportunity to look within yourself. It will help you push past your comfort zone and become a different version of yourself that you never thought was possible.

I want to take a step back for a moment and explain how an Englishman found himself co-founding a run club in the heart of West Hollywood, and ultimately how I came to meet Brady. I have been running for many years and used to race half marathons, marathons, and triathlons in the UK.

Running for me, always driven by my ego, was about how fast I could run and how much quicker I could be in every race. I consistently pushed myself in training and races. And eventually, it took its toll on me when I woke up in a hospital in Las Vegas! I passed out from dehydration between mile eleven and twelve of the Rock N' Roll half marathon. This prompted me to look deep inside and remember the reason I got hooked on running - for the fun and love of it! Running has done so much for me, both physically and mentally. After living in Los Angeles for a couple of years, I felt the urge to bring people together to share a laugh, meet new friends, raise each other's vibrations and get stronger in the mind and body. After being introduced to Dee Murthy through a mutual friend, we co-founded the Grand Running Club in LA. We would meet at Melrose Place every Saturday morning and would consistently get a good turnout of young like-minded entrepreneurial guys and girls. With it being LA, we would regularly see people come through with a hangover and then never see them again.

Then along came Brady one Saturday morning, still slightly buzzed from the previous night's antics. He was wide eyed and probably wondering why he was joining a bunch of energized happy folks on a Saturday morning about to run up and down the hills through West Hollywood and Beverly Hills!

I remember thinking Brady had a good energy about him but didn't necessarily expect to see him again after he coughed and sputtered his way around the three mile route. I texted our running community every Thursday to remind and invite them to run club. For weeks, Brady responded with random excuses as to why he couldn't make it.

Then, one Saturday, he showed up again. Eventually, he was consistently showing up. He started showing up for himself. Thereafter, Brady became an integral part of our run club community. It was amazing to see the changes and growth in Brady as he made it a habit to run. He started to get curious about what he could really do with his body and mind. A half marathon, full marathon, and half-ironman later, Brady showed up to run club one morning in April of 2019 with an announcement to make. He put his arm around me and told our community that he was leaving the next month to head to the east coast and run across America to San Diego!

It blew my mind. So many thoughts ran through my head (no pun intended!), but I had one prevalent thought - I knew he would make it. When he left LA and flew out east, I remember thinking how he really wasn't messing around and was super serious about this massive journey. It was almost instant from when he announced it to when he started his first run from the pier in New Jersey.

I don't know if it was some sense of responsibility I felt for getting Brady into running, but I really wanted to support him every step of the way. I would send him daily text messages in the mornings to keep his spirits and energy high. I'd always send something from the heart so he knew we were thinking of him everyday.

It then became the norm every Saturday morning for me to let everyone know how many miles he'd run, and which state and city he was in. It gave everyone perspective on what he was going through before we would start our runs! Sometimes we would FaceTime him in the middle of our Saturday morning run club runs. I would always look forward to seeing his daily updates on social media.

It was a very special moment when my wife, myself, and a group from our run community flew out to run with him in Nashville, Tennessee. It was mid July and about a third of the way through his epic run. Then, in early December, the weekend of Brady's final run in San Diego, a large group of our community ventured south to join him for his last miles on that Sunday.

I remember the night before his final run, my wife, Riley from the run club, and myself went out to meet Brady at his parents house. We had the opportunity to interview him on our podcast on the eve of his last run. It was an incredibly honest and humbling conversation. He talked through the ups and downs of an unbelievable journey with Nate, his co-pilot and RV driver, and told some great anecdotes.

Running alongside Brady on his last miles into the Pacific Ocean is a memory I look back on with love. Since Brady became a running legend for going across America Forrest Gump style, he's consistently surprised me with his newest escapades. But, I don't want to give away any spoilers, so you'll have to read on!

Brady's determination, drive and desire is infectious. It equally matches his big smile, lust and love for life! Whenever I receive a text from Brady, I immediately know it's going to be something awesome and inspiring. I am excited for you to read, feel, and be ignited by Brady's journey across America and adventures beyond. If you ever get the opportunity to meet Brady during one of his speaking engagements or at a book signing, be sure to soak up his wisdom, energy, and any advice he might pass your way. He's a special person and I'm grateful to call him my brother from another mother.

Luke embracing Brady on the final day across USA

Preface

Hello there! I am honored that you found this book. I wrote and published the first attempt of this book in 2020 after finishing a 3,311 mile and 218 day run across the USA. Since then, I've been inspired to share more about my life experience, including many things I haven't shared publicly with others. This book is my opportunity to give a little more. If this book can help one person take one step towards their dream, it has served its purpose.

So what type of book is *It all starts with one step*? Consider this a playbook for following your dreams! Each play has been patiently crafted and tested. These plays have helped me find a lot of success, joy, fulfillment, faith, hope, and peace in my life. Many of the lessons I share in this book were earned through my personal life experiences involving blood, sweat, and tears.

If that isn't enough for you, I also include many stories that have inspired me throughout my life, which all support the lessons I share with you. I include stories from war, business, baseball and many other places and things. Every play you will read about is ingrained in me and my goal is to pass them on to you.

In sports, a playbook is only helpful if you put the plays into action and practice them. Which is why I have incorporated exercises at the end of every chapter to act as a catalyst for change. My hope for you is that you don't just read the plays from this book - but you practice the plays in your own life.

Imagine that you are standing at the base of a metaphorical mountain and your dream is waiting for you at the summit. You can move towards your dream or stay on the ground level and wonder, "What lies above the clouds?" I hope you choose to take a step towards your dreams with me. Let's get it!

God Bless, Brady

CHAPTER 1

WE CAN'T HAVE ROSES
WITHOUT THORNS

D o you believe in overnight successes? I don't. Chances are that trendy new entrepreneur, actor, or author has been at it for years. Let's start with one entrepreneur that was probably called an overnight success at some point. This young man I am referring to grew up in Hangzhou, China. Following his graduation from college, he applied for thirty different jobs, and was denied work from every single employer. Amongst his rejections was the fast food restaurant chain, KFC. The man who couldn't even get hired by KFC was named Jack Ma. Jack went on to start a global B2B marketplace called Alibaba, and Mr. Ma is now worth over twenty-four billion dollars [1].

Now, on to an actor whose dream took many years to blossom. As a fifteen-year-old boy he dropped out of high school to get a job as a janitor to support his family. His dream was to pursue comedy professionally but during his first stand-up show he got booed off of the stage. He auditioned for Saturday Night Live in 1980-81 but didn't land a role. This man I am referring to is Jim Carrey, who is now regarded as one of the greatest comedians of all time [2].

Lastly, let's discuss a trendy new author that "got lucky" and was once divorced and living on financial aid. Everything was riding on a fantasy novel she had been working on for years. After three years of looking for a publishing deal, her book was rejected by twelve publishers. Finally, one small publisher gave the book a chance after the CEO's daughter fell in love with it. The author of that book was J.K Rowling and the book was the first of the Harry Potter series [3].

In 2024, following your dream can seem fun, euphoric and magical. Social media circulates stories of success and happiness while often leaving out the behind the scenes reality of what it takes to follow your dream. Following a dream can be crushing mentally and physically. Our perception of success needs to change. When we see someone's success we can only see half of the full picture. The typical social media post doesn't highlight real life struggle. Below the surface, we face constant obstacles while working towards what we want to achieve.

Everyone wants to be successful and reach their dreams. However, not everyone will put in the time, effort, and dedication to make it a reality. We can have food, clothing, and practically anything shipped to our doorstep in minutes, but we need to remember that achieving our dreams is not at all that simple. There will be constant road bumps on our journey and when we learn to accept that, the better off we will be.

If J.K Rowling had the perception that her road to success would be smooth sailing, the first publisher rejection would have ended her career. Instead, Rowlings accepted all of the negative and positive outcomes that came along with chasing her dream. That mentality is what helped her become one of the most accomplished writers of our time.

There will be constant road bumps on our journey...

I still remember the day I launched my company, Sunny Co Clothing, at The University of Arizona. We only had one person buy our product and she was a friend of ours. It wasn't the most glamorous launch day. If we expected to sell thousands of products immediately and become an overnight success, we wouldn't have stuck with it.

Luckily, we believed in our product and brand. We understood that patience was our secret ingredient. Unlike the pre-cut roses you receive at the store, we understood that real roses come with prickly thorns. About eight months later, we had a bouquet of roses when we received 50,000 orders in twenty-eight minutes. I learned that you can't receive thousands of roses without receiving thousands of thorns.

Entering into my running era, I knew I would get the occasional thorn in my shoe. For a long time, running was not fun, euphoric, or magical for me whatsoever. From a young age I actually hated running. No, that was not a typo. You understood that right. I used to hate running. I was the kid in class that would fake being sick to get out of running the mile in PE class.

My favorite sport growing up was soccer. When I was twelve years old, my competitive soccer team was called Attack. At the end of the year party, I heard rumors that we would have to run even more the following season. Just hearing that was enough for me to tell my parents I was quitting. Pretty ironic, huh? Near the end of 2018 my roommate Taylor convinced me to join a running club. I was hesitant because I didn't view myself as much of a runner. More importantly, I still hated running! However, Taylor was quite convincing, so I decided to go to the club to be social and meet new people.

I remember on the way to the club thinking to myself, "What if I run weird? What if I can't run the miles everyone else can?" I was not a runner, nor did I even look at myself as an athlete. When I first went, I could barely run the three miles that were expected of us. I felt like a fish out of water. It was really difficult for me. At this time, my running journey was only thorns. My first smell of roses came in November of 2018. I completed my first half marathon and it completely changed the way I viewed running. I became curious about what I was capable of, mentally and physically. Before this experience, I never familiarized myself with running lingo because I never thought I would be able to run marathons.

Fast forward to May 31, 2019. I was in Fairfax, Virginia on Day 27 of my USA run and nearing the 300 mile mark. I was dealing with a lot of toe nail pain. I ended up ripping off my toe nail, skin attached. If this hasn't happened to you before, all you need to know is that this hurts, really bad. As you could guess, this was a thorny experience for me. The pain was rough and it got worse when I put pressure on my foot. I found myself complaining most of that morning. I didn't realize how poor my attitude was until we met a woman in a parking lot named Rose.

I was not a runner, nor did I even look at myself as an athlete.

Her energy was glowing and she radiated warmth. As an immigrant from Italy, Rose shared her enthusiasm and pride with us for living in the USA. She even gifted me a beautiful woven scarf with the American flag on it. As we parted ways, something hit me. While I had a piss poor attitude at the time, in front of me was Rose with a beautiful perspective on life.

I realized in that moment, if I wanted to be successful, that I could no longer complain on the run. No one forced me to run across the country, I had chosen to undertake this challenge myself. I needed to start taking complete responsibility for my journey. From that day forward, I welcomed and honored every rose and thorn that came from the experience. These thorns I mention did not shy away from me on the journey!

One thorn that really stood out was near Oklahoma City. I didn't share this with anyone on social media at the time because it was personal and very gross. I was frightened for my health, so I kept it private. For some context, I was running around eighteen miles a day at this point in the run. Although the summer heat of Oklahoma was brutal, I felt good.

It was Day 131, and something caught me by surprise when I went to the bathroom in the RV. Although I felt fine, it was clear to me that I had just urinated blood. I had never experienced this before in my life and I was really concerned for my health. We were over half way done with the cross country run but still had about ninety days left. I hoped this was related to the extreme amounts of running I was doing, and not something else. I imagined it could have been caused by dehydration, but the fear of the unknown was scary. I did what most of us do and searched WebMD, which only made my concerns worse. I took a gamble and decided the cause was dehydration, so I hydrated excessively for the next couple of days. It occurred again the next night, but after that it finally went away. I would definitely consider pissing blood as a thorn.

What came with a few thorns were so many roses: Surprising my grandma at her retirement home in Pennsylvania. Country artist Charles Wesley Godwin shouting me out in West Virginia. My run club visiting me in Nashville, Tennessee. Running a marathon in Memphis, followed by eating barbecue and watching live blues at BB Kings. Mike Posner reaching out to me on social media and connecting with him throughout the run. Meeting the famously kind police officer Mr. Norman in Little Rock, Arkansas. Ryan Seacrest interviewing me state by state from Texas to California. My parents, friends, and family surprising me several times on the run. Watching the endless sky of stars at night in the Arizona desert. My running videos being shared by SportsCenter and watched by millions of people on Tik Tok. One of my inspirations and MVP Super Bowl Champion Ray Lewis, sending me a video message on my birthday. Hundreds of friends and family joining me on that final day in San Diego.

The list of roses from my experience could go on and on and on. Every rose was worth every single thorn. I might not have welcomed the thorns immediately, but looking back, the thorns made the journey that much sweeter. The roses were the good times throughout the journey. The thorns were the times that I knew could either make or break me. Marshall Sylver once said, "The greater the responsibility, the greater the reward." Oftentimes, as our opportunity for rewards increase, our responsibilities and risk increases too.

Every rose was worth every single thorn.

If we want the greatest rewards in life, we need to be ready to overcome the greatest obstacles along the way. Denzel Washington explains this concept with a popular African proverb in the movie *The Equalizer*. He says, "You pray for rain, you gotta deal with the mud." What a profound line! We all want success and good times to pour down on us. We just don't want to get our shoes wet and dirty. If you are ready for everything that comes with following your dreams, then follow your dream.

Don't pray for the rain if you aren't ready for what the rain will bring. When following your dream gets hard, and it will get hard, remember you are the one that chose to sign up. Alibaba exists despite Ma's thirty job rejections. *Dumb and Dumber* and the legendary comedian Jim Carrey exist despite getting booed off stage. The Harry Potter series exists despite the twelve publishers that rejected Rowlings. My historic run only exists because of what I learned when I ripped off my toe nail in Virginia.

There are lessons in every thorn. Don't be afraid to get your shoes muddy. You can handle the mud.

WE CAN'T HAVE ROSES WITHOUT THORNS

Brady and Rose meeting in Virginia

EXERCISE:

What is one thorn you've faced while chasing a dream?

_____

_____

_____

_____

_____

What is one rose you have experienced while chasing a dream?

_____

_____

_____

_____

_____

What is one way you can better approach your thorns and roses?

_____

_____

_____

_____

_____

CHAPTER 2

UNDERTHINK IT

We make so many decisions throughout the day, more than we even realize. For example, if you are reading this right now that means you made a financial decision to purchase this book or someone decided to give it to you. If someone gifted it to you, you are very lucky. If you purchased it yourself, maybe you had to log onto Amazon.com. Before that, you pulled out your phone, kindle, or laptop. And by buying this book, perhaps you opted out of purchasing something else, another decision.

You see where I am going with this. We make decisions without even thinking about them sometimes. You know this when you drive a familiar route and then all of a sudden you are at your destination and you don't remember much of the drive (hence the phrase autopilot).

We wouldn't get much done if we spent hours and hours overthinking every little decision throughout the day. For me, I find peace when I trust my gut instinct. If I do that, it allows me to avoid looking back on what could have been. One of my overarching goals is to live life without regrets. The only time I experience regret is when I don't trust my gut instinct.

In 2019, my gut told me to run across the United States of America. Choosing to run across America is a tough decision and requires more thought than choosing between dairy, oat or almond milk at your local cafe. But my question to you is this, does deciding whether to follow your dream have to be such a troublesome decision? Sometimes we overthink a goal or a dream just to come up with an excuse to not follow it.

For example, let's imagine that you and your friend planned to run a marathon together. While you are supposed to be training, someone sends you a video of a runner exhausted on the ground after a race. You start to go down a rabbit hole of thoughts about the pain, difficulty, and duration of the race. You begin to feel anxious and decide you'd rather just watch from the sidelines. So, you make up some story to your friend about how you are busy that weekend. Our dreams can evaporate instantly just like that.

Whenever the worst case scenario floods our mind, the risk can seem too great to overcome. Our dreams fall down like trees in a forest. While the world might not see it happen, it still makes a sound that we can hear. The sound of us not following our dreams is deafening. It haunts us to know that we let our dreams slip away. And why? Because while we were thinking of everything that could go wrong, we could have gotten to work.

There are endless reasons why we overthink our dreams. It could be imposter syndrome, lack of experience, fear of failure, or another lie. One reason we overthink our dreams is because we look at someone successful and forget that they too started from somewhere. We tell ourselves we need to know everything from the start and we need to find success immediately.

The sound of us not following our dreams is deafening.

Some of the most successful people I have met in my life have all shared one thing in common, they didn't have all the answers from the beginning. We all fall down, especially the successful ones. Successful people get back up the quickest after so-called "failures." They "underthink it" and they focus on action.

We put entrepreneurs, politicians, athletes, scholars, musicians and people alike on pedestals. We act like these people were always as great as they are today. Stop reading for a second and google search the image of the Amazon offices in 1999 and you will understand my point. It looks like their logo at the time was made by a graffiti artist. Just like Amazon, every company and every person starts from somewhere.

Before running across the country, I had one experience that exemplified the "underthink it" mindset. It came during my 2015 summer study abroad trip in Buenos Aires, Argentina. We had a guest speaker come into our class one day who was one of the co-founders of a well-known global shoe brand. I was really excited to hear from him and wanted to learn what it was like to start a globally successful brand.

I didn't know what to expect, but I definitely did not expect to relate to his talk on a personal level. He shared a story about a shipment of shoes they received. Time was limited, so they had to test the durability and quality of the shoes without too much thinking. While one of the founders was inside a bank taking care of business, the other founder ran circles outside in the shoes.

When I heard this story, it was like the veil of success had been removed. I could relate to this story. I could relate to these guys. They seemed silly and reminded me of myself. I could imagine myself in their shoes running around the bank. They approached this problem with a simple solution and something that anyone, including myself, could do.

When we put people on pedestals, we create a barrier between us and them. Subconsciously, we tell ourselves that we could never rise to that level of greatness because we are so far below them anyways. Are these businesses and people that much more special and gifted than you or I? Aren't we all special? Maybe greatness is within every single one of us and we just need to find it. Finding it demands action and courage.

I really didn't do all that much training leading up to the big run. I finished my first half marathon (13.1 miles) seven months prior to the USA run and I finished my first full marathon (26.2 miles) only two months prior. Despite my lack of running experience, I was convinced that I could run 3,000 miles. How? I broke it down as simply as I could. If the USA was about 3,000 miles wide, and I ran ten miles per day, I would finish in about 300 days. While I was strategizing, I was averaging only three miles per day. When I wrote down the idea to run across America in my journal, I thought of what I needed to accomplish this new dream of mine.

Maybe greatness is within every single one of us and we just need to find it.

First, I would need somewhere to sleep at night (an RV). Second, I would need someone to drive and offer crew support (my friend Nate Hiser). Third, I would need money to pay for everything (my savings). Then, I would need to find a safe route to navigate (Google Maps walking directions). Oh, and last but not least, I would have to find the courage to run over 3,000 miles, which turned out to be 3,311 - probably due to my lack of navigation skills.

I felt like an underdog before running across the country. Who doesn't like a good underdog story? To prevent psyching myself out of a challenge only 337 people completed before me, I kept my research around the subject to a minimum. I was ready to make a figurative leap of faith and the last thing I wanted was paralysis analysis.

Before beginning my run in New Jersey, I visited my friends Brandon and Ariana in New York. To prepare for my journey ahead, we decided to go to a bookstore. I headed to the running section and will never forget what happened next. I picked up a book that said something along the lines of, "How to Run Really Far." I read a few pages and my mind instantly started to race with doubts and fears that hadn't come up before. I quickly put the book down and left the store. Just like the shoe founders, I needed to simplify and run around the bank. I needed to "underthink it."

I figured out everything on the go. I spent the first few weeks mapping out my route on Google Maps. Nate knew where I was running to for the day, so he would wait there for me. Google Maps limits walking directions to about 300 miles at a time, so I never had the entire 3,311 mile route planned out. As the trip continued, the route became more and more flexible. A few months in, I stopped planning where I would finish my runs for the day. Instead, I would just choose my distance during a run and then text Nate my location when I finished. Nate and I usually didn't plan where to park our RV for the night until after I finished my run for the day. Luckily, there are a lot of Walmarts, Dollar Generals, and churches around the country that let us stay overnight in their parking lots. It always worked itself out.

Life is a lot simpler than we make it. Sometimes we overcomplicate things and think about future problems that don't exist. If you are brand new to running, perhaps you should buy a pair of running shoes before binge watching videos about one hundred mile ultra races. Simplify, simplify, simplify.

Sometimes we overcomplicate things and think about future problems that don't exist.

Don't forget that before my big run, I was only averaging three miles per day. Guess how many miles I was running in the final two months across the country? Twenty miles per day! Whatever your dream is, think about the simplest way to get started, and get moving. Remember, I never read that book on how to run really far… and if I had, who knows if I'd be writing this book today.

UNDERTHINK IT

Nate (left) and Brady (right), standing next to RV just days before USA run

Brady walking the pier at Bayshore Waterfront Park in NJ before starting journey across the country

EXERCISE:

What is one dream in your life that you think you could approach more simply?

_____

_____

_____

_____

_____

What is one thing you can do today to put your dream into action?

_____

_____

_____

_____

_____

What will it mean to you when you achieve this dream? What will it feel like?

_____

_____

_____

_____

_____

CHAPTER 3

RUN LIKE ZENYATTA

Have you ever been inspired to do something and then one Google search later you talked yourself out of it? "Be more realistic," you might have told yourself. It can feel sometimes like the world is just waiting to spit in the face of your dream. One of the first dreams I remember having as a kid was to be an ice cream truck driver. I was eight years old, don't judge me! As you could imagine, I was met with a lot of laughter from my friends and family.

From a young age we are told what we can and can't do. We are told what is possible for us and what is impossible. And although we are well intentioned, a lot of us can steer others away from their dreams with our feedback. Whenever I personally share dreams or goals with friends or family, it is usually to see if their enthusiasm matches mine. We wait to see how someone else responds and if they don't encourage us to follow that dream, we might quickly find ourselves saying something like, "You are right! What was I thinking?"

When I started Sunny Co Clothing with my friend Alan, it was our senior year at The University of Arizona. During graduation, we were asked to stand up if we had started a company. Alan and I were standing with maybe three more students in my graduating class of 700 students that day. You could say that what Alan and I were doing wasn't the norm.

It was typical of our business school to host a job fair during the semester so that students could line up jobs after college. One of my teachers insisted that every student in our class attend. Alan and I were having a lot of success with the company, so I was hesitant. For me, it just seemed like a back up plan. My teacher called me out during class one day because he knew I didn't want to go to the job fair. He went on to share the statistics of how many startups fail within the first year. In a sense, he was making a joke out of my dream in front of my friends and classmates. Luckily, our company had found much success at the time, so I brushed off his comment and kept working towards my goals. But what if I hadn't been this confident? What is now a global swimwear brand that is sold in department stores across the whole country, Sunny Co Clothing, might not even exist.

After deciding to run across America in March of 2019, I didn't tell another soul about the idea for a full month. I wanted to give myself some time to reflect on the dream without outside input. Finally, in early April, I started telling friends and family. My roommate Xander had a wonderful reaction. We used to walk across the street from our apartment to a restaurant called B'koah. Naturally, he said, "Bro you're a psycho, I don't even like walking to B'Koah."

When I shared the news with my dad, he initially tried to talk me out of it. His intentions were coming from a place of concern and love but his reaction still confused me. He said, "You haven't posted about this on social media yet, you can still back out." Looking back, my dad was just being a protective parent. With that being said, who knows how his words would have affected me if I didn't keep the idea to myself for that first month.

We are all familiar with the phrase, "Sticks and stones may break my bones, but words will never hurt me." Most of us would agree with this quote but why do we still give so much power to the words of those around us? Our dreams are for us. They are ours. No one can tell you whether you should or shouldn't follow your dream. Well, they can try to tell you that. But, you have the power to control whether or not their words affect you. If you are going to tell somebody your dreams, be ready to hear something you don't like. Be ready for the sticks and stones.

Our dreams are for us.

When you are ready to receive feedback, remember that someone's opinion is a reflection of their life experience. Let's say that you want to become a scuba diver! You are really excited about it and you share the news with your sister. However, your sister watched Shark Week at a very young age and is completely terrified of the ocean.

You have to take your sister's feedback with a grain of salt. Her opinion might not be encouraging given her own experience with the ocean. We have to keep blinders on when it comes to outside opinions. And when we offer feedback to others, we must keep in mind our delivery, so we don't discourage them from following their dream.

In addition to outside noise from others, you must beware of the noise in your own head. I remember before running across the USA I would look at myself in the mirror and say, "You can do this." Those little pep talks really helped. One of my favorite quotes from Confucius says, "The man who says he can and the man who says he can't are both correct." At the end of the day, what you are capable of is up to you, nobody else.

Before the trip across America, my friend Nate and I gave a nickname to our RV, Zenyatta. Zenyatta is one of the greatest horses to have ever raced. Zenyatta wrapped her career up with nineteen first place wins and one second place finish in her final race [4]. She lost her last race by three inches [5]. If you watch any of Zenyatta's nineteen victories online, you will quickly catch on to her strategy. She always ran faster and faster towards the end of each race. She could be dead last for most of a race and finish in first place every time, shocking every person in attendance.

The reason I have always resonated with this horse and her story is because she raced differently. More specifically, Zenyatta ran her own race. She never worried about the other horses who ran ahead of her. She unapologetically ran at her own pace. If life was considered a race, should you run at your own pace? Or should you run faster or slower based on the other runners around you?

When I was in high school I found myself running someone else's race, literally. During high school football tryouts, we all had to run a forty yard dash as they called it. I lined up and got ready to run as fast as I could. Instead of focusing on my strides and my strides only, I noticed the runner next to me was running faster than me. I got nervous and started running out of my shoes. I stopped running my own race and was punished for it. As unbelievable as it sounds, I pulled my hamstring at the end of the sprint. The pressure got to me. I let the person running next to me change how I pursued my dream. We can chase our dreams or we can let others chase them for us.

I stopped running my own race and
was punished for it.

Maybe your mother or father don't believe in your dream and you don't want to disappoint them, so you work a job that you hate. Maybe your partner wants you to get a serious job to support your family but you find meaning in the work you do. We can't run our own race if we are constantly running someone else's. Don't focus on where everyone else is on the track. Meditate on your dream and believe in it. Approach the starting gate.

Alan Alchalel (left) and Brady selling their swimwear
at The University of Arizona bookstore

EXERCISE:

In the past, have you let the feedback of others stop you from following one of your dreams? What was the result?

_____

_____

_____

_____

_____

_____

Is the feedback of others necessary for you to achieve your dream?

_____

_____

_____

_____

_____

_____

CHAPTER 4

BREAK FREE OF YOUR SHELL

L obsters grow in a very peculiar way. Lobsters go through a process of change called molting, Which simply means that when a Lobster grows, it must break out of its current shell in order to grow into a bigger shell [6]. This process is supposedly very painful and involves a lot of stress. Unfortunately, there is no way around it. If they do not shed their shell, they will not grow.

How is this process any different from humans? Don't we all need to shed our old ways to grow into our better selves? If nothing ever changes and we just stay the same, won't that hinder our growth? One constant we can count on that facilitates this shedding process is change. There is a great quote by Heraclitus that says, "No man ever steps in the same river twice, for it is not the same river and he is not the same man." Change is painful. Naturally, I do what a lot of us do at times and try to avoid change in my life. Believe it or not, you can't outrun change - take that from someone who ran thousands and thousands of miles.

In a perfect existence, I would embrace change with a smile at

If they do not shed their shell, they will not grow.

every corner. But since I am human and far from perfect, welcoming change can be complicated. Whether it was the weather, the terrain, or the size of the towns, change was something I could rely on across the USA. Everything always changed. We experienced change throughout every step of the journey.

It was Day 103 and I was just crossing over the Mississippi River into Arkansas. Nate was on the bridge to snap a video of me running by. I ran over hundreds of bridges across the country, and if you followed my journey on social media you probably heard me shout "another bridge" all the time. This was the most dangerous bridge I ran over because I only had one foot of running room between the barrier and the cars driving by. I was able to cross the bridge safely into Arkansas, but I knew something didn't feel right. As I kept running, I felt discomfort in my left achilles tendon.

Up until this point of the run, I experienced all types of pain. Ankle pain, calf pain, foot pain, hamstring pain, hip pain, etc - you get the point! I would notice the pain and then tend to it after my runs with extra recovery. Although this pain wasn't really different from anything else I experienced, my mind played tricks on me and this potential injury shook me to my core. I tried to keep running after feeling the discomfort in my tendon but my left leg started to go limp. My usual "jog it off" routine wasn't going to work this time. I ended up walking for the remainder of that day and did my best to take care of my leg in recovery.

The next morning was rough, but I was still able to get out there and walk for eighteen miles. I was really struggling mentally and physically on Day 105 (two days into the achilles pain). I woke up and my right leg was in pain, which was probably a result of overcompensating on my right side. Around this time, I had a conversation with my dad about the situation. My pops was looking out for my safety and reminded me that if I overdid it, the trip would be over. Our conversation made me wonder if I should continue.

I remember when we stopped talking, I started crying. And I mean really crying. I had put every single piece of myself into this run and was nearing 1,400 miles total. I was almost halfway through the entire challenge and the thought of not finishing it terrified me. I felt powerless. I felt hopeless.

Our conversation made me wonder if I should continue.

I remember some of the initial thoughts that went through my head. "Why me? Why is this happening to me?" Looking back now, it is clear that I was rejecting this giant obstacle of change in my way. I was doing everything right. Stretching, recovering strong, giving it 110% effort and even raising money for charity. This experience showed me that you can give your everything in life, and still come up short on your goals. Just like Tom Hanks famously quoted in *Forrest Gump*, sometimes in life, "**** happens." I knew there was nothing left to do but accept the situation and move forward as best I could.

Instead of running from this tornado of change in front of me, I needed to go through it. I needed to break my shell. I ended up taking rest days on Days 106 and 107. We were parked outside a Dollar General, and I didn't leave the RV for two days. I wasn't going to do anything to make the situation at hand worse. On Day 108, I felt like I was ready to test out the weak leg and achilles tendon. I leaned on Nate, family, friends and supporters, and I said prayers. I really didn't know if the tendon was going to hold up. There was a chance it could tear on the spot. I had Nate film my first few strides and I remember telling him to keep filming no matter what happened. I took about three steps, looked up at Nate, and gave him a thumbs up. We were back in business! Following that day, I ran for forty days in a row before taking a rest day in Amarillo, Texas.

Someone who has experienced and embraced vast change in his life is Navy SEAL, ultrarunner, and best selling author, David Goggins. David was once working paycheck to paycheck as a pest exterminator and weighed 300 pounds [7]. He realized his life needed drastic change or else he would be stuck in a miserable existence for the rest of his life. David decided he wanted to not just join the military but become a Navy SEAL, one of the most elite fighting forces in the world. Goggins went on to achieve that dream and many others, such as finishing The Badwater 135, a 135 mile race in Death Valley and one of the toughest races in the world. In his book, *Can't Hurt Me*, Goggins highlights the depths of suffering that he climbed out of. One thing that Goggins talks about in his book is something he calls the "Cookie Jar." This jar is full of challenges that you have gone through in your life and overcame. And the idea is that when you go through anything hard again, you remember those challenges you once overcame and you know deep down you can do it again.

Overcoming my achilles injury became the single biggest cookie in my cookie jar during the USA run. I felt as if I had defeated Goliath when I overcame that injury. No matter what came my way on the run, I remembered how I fought through that challenge. When everything seemed like it was against me, I was able to keep going. I knew that I overcame an insurmountable circumstance and I could do it again.

After 150 days across the USA, the running was starting to catch up to me. I was in Texas and remember feeling an overwhelming pain in my legs following my daily runs. The pain was brutal. I was in so much pain that the only time I was able to feel relief was when I went to sleep at night.

My practice of RICE (rest, ice, compression, elevation) was not helping and I decided to turn to anti-inflammatory options. I took

Advil a lot growing up when I had pain, so I returned to the habit. I think at one point I was taking something like twelve pills of Advil daily for the pain. For reference, I don't think it's recommended to take more than six tablets of Advil in one day. I did anything possible to get rid of the pain. I started to take Tylenol (extra strength) as well and nothing helped. I was looking for a quick fix to an issue that clearly had deep roots. I was trying to avoid the problem.

I was in so much pain that the only time I was able to feel relief was when I went to sleep at night.

I was not ready to accept that the pain I was feeling was not going away anytime soon. I finally decided to stop taking the anti-inflammatory pills and accepted the situation I was in. I accepted that pain was going to be a part of the journey, and what happened after was incredible. The pain felt like it subsided. For the rest of my journey, it was still slightly there but it was not as powerful as it once was. There is a great quote by the renowned Swiss psychiatrist Carl Jung that I thought about during this experience. The quote says, "Whatever you resist persists." The longer I resisted the pain the worse it became.

Why do we resist change so much? We are all capable of overcoming the greatest of life's challenges and yet, we still find ourselves fearful of the situation we are in. Change scares me personally because change is new. "What if I am not equipped to handle change this time?" I ask myself. My mind is good at messing with me. When I am faced with a new major challenge I like to reflect on everything I have overcome in my past. Every challenge looks different, but the mindset that is required of me to overcome these challenges doesn't look different at all. I know what I am capable of. I know that when my back is against the wall, I will fight and find a way to overcome what is in front of me.

I will always remember what my friend and crewmate Nate said to me during the achilles scare in Arkansas. He said, "This is going to make the finish in San Diego that much sweeter." Nate was right, it really did. And when we finally got to San Diego, I immediately got a tattoo of my route across the country. Where did I put the tattoo? I put it over my Achilles tendon injury from Arkansas. That injury was a catalyst for growth on my run. Change was necessary for me to complete my journey.

The accomplished and hilarious comedian, Theo Von, once said, "Nothing Changes If Nothing Changes." I once heard somewhere that most people who sign up for weight loss programs do so after their seatbelt won't click in. Whenever a giant obstacle is standing right in front us, it is hard to deny its existence. It is no longer a hypothetical situation. The obstacle in front of you is real, and the first thing you need to do is acknowledge it's there. We can't defeat an enemy that is unnamed. Then, when you are ready to face these challenges, remember your ability to overcome change, and face it head on. We can then learn from change and grow from the experience. Don't wait until your seat belt doesn't click in to accept change.

The Brady that touched the Atlantic Ocean in New Jersey on Day 1 was not the same Brady that jumped into the Pacific Ocean on Day 218 in California. Change was essential to my experience. We become fearful when we are faced with new life changes.

...remember your ability to overcome change.

Change is one of the few things in life that is guaranteed. We can either face it or we can hide from it. Hiding from change doesn't make our situations go away. Like a student procrastinating to study for an exam, the exam is still going to be given. The highly regarded Irish singer/songwriter Dermot Kennedy sings, "We've had problems that we've grown through," in his song, "An Evening I Will Not Forget." Like Dermot's wise words, I didn't just go through change on my USA run, I grew through change. My problems are not going anywhere and neither are yours. If we want to grow, there is only one way through. We must be like the lobster and break our shells.

BREAK FREE OF YOUR SHELL

Brady walking on injured achilles tendon in Arkansas

Today is Day 105. So much has changed in the last 48 hours. My left achilles tendon started to hurt midway through my run on Thursday. I didn't think too much of it until yesterday when it felt about 50%. I ended up walking 18 miles and it wasn't easy but my legs managed. Last night I spoke with my dad about everything and he reminded me of the big picture + I have at least over 100 days left out here. If I over do it and really injure my achilles the whole run could be over. After we hung up I got emotional and cried for the first time in awhile. I thought about everything I've sacrificed to be out here and all the hours I've worked my ass off out here to get to this moment. I'd be lying if I said I wasn't scared right now. I want this so bad. I really don't know what

Brady's journal entry from Day 105 of running across America

EXERCISE:

What is one major life change you have gone through and overcome in your life?

_____

_____

_____

_____

_____

What is one habit in your life that you are resisting to change? How is
it holding you back from your dream?

_____

_____

_____

_____

_____

What is one new habit you can add to your routine to create positive
change?

_____

_____

_____

_____

_____

CHAPTER 5

NOT ALL PROBLEMS ARE BAD

When Alan and I founded our clothing company, we were brand new to business. Since our dads were both entrepreneurs, we constantly asked them for advice. After our company went viral (the red swimsuit from Instagram), we experienced all types of problems. First, we had to switch manufacturers because we received 50,000 orders in twenty-eight minutes. Then, our Instagram account got shut down because they thought we were a bot account since we gained 780,000 followers in one day. And on top of all that, we had TMZ calling us five times a day for a week!

I remember when I told my dad all this he said, "Those are good problems." I was so confused. But then he explained, "You're switching manufacturers because you have more orders than you did last month, your Instagram shut down because you have more fans than you did last month, and TMZ is calling you because you have more people talking about your company than you did last month." His word choice is what struck me. I didn't know there could be "good problems." I just thought all problems were bad. This lesson stuck with me during my run across America.

I raised 42,000 dollars for eleven different charities throughout my run including Make-A-Wish, Wounded Warrior Project, and Foster Nation to name a few. I would highlight each charity every few weeks while I was running across the country. My problems seemed tiny compared to kids fighting cancer, veterans fighting mental health issues, and foster youth fighting to stay out of jail. I can't remember who said this to me on my run, but they said, "Brady, people would kill to have your problems." I reminded myself of this each time I was on the verge of complaining.

Without being aware, the words we use can frame our personal experiences. What we tell ourselves about our problems and duties on a day to day basis sincerely affects us. Shifting the way I look at my problems transformed my entire perspective throughout the cross country run. Instead of telling myself "I have" to run every day, I told myself "I get" to do this. The distinction between "have" and "get" changed my whole perspective during each run. When we reshape the way we see our personal struggles, it allows us to be more grateful for what we have.

In an effort to maintain this mindset, I began to add a special routine to my daily run. I would consider the first mile of every run a "grateful mile." Every day, I ran the first mile without listening to music or podcasts, and all I would think about were the things I was grateful for. Since I am not a super fast runner, this went on for eight to twelve minutes. I would say things out loud like, "Thank you God for my breath, thank you for my sight, thank you for my hearing, thank you for my health, thank you for my energy…" When you run in nature without headphones or distractions, there are so many beautiful things that can come to our mind. Nature alone is something we can all be grateful for and in awe over.

The grateful mile practice became a wonderful foundation for every run. I looked at every day on the cross country run as an opportunity. I would much rather tackle opportunities every day instead of problems. Opportunities are much better than problems, right? If I thought of every run as a problem that needed to be solved, I would have constantly felt like a firefighter putting out flames. No matter what I was dealing with on any given day, I found so many things to be grateful for. And if I could get through that first mile, I could get through the next mile and the one after that.

On Day 80 in Gallatin, Tennessee I surpassed the 1,000 mile mark. This accomplishment meant so much to me. I needed to celebrate it in a big way. To celebrate this feat I decided to donate 1,000 dollars for 1,000 miles. I wanted to give the money to a person that my fans felt was deserving. Out of all the suggestions that came in, one really spoke to me.

I would much rather tackle opportunities

every day instead of problems.

I was introduced to a story about a man named Josh Woodward. Josh was a firefighter, husband, and father to two kids. What seemed like an ordinary cut for Josh became a life-threatening infection. His body went through something called sepsis. Basically, the chemicals that our body releases to fight an infection started to become inflamed for Josh. The doctors gave Josh a five percent chance of living through the night.Imagine those odds for a second.

Josh and his family took that five percent chance, and they clung to hope. Despite all odds, Josh survived that night! This story about Josh and his family gave me so much strength and inspiration on my run. If I started to think about how my feet felt sore, I would think of him and how some don't have the same luxury of complaining about foot pain.

We all have problems in our life. For some reason, our individual problems can seem way bigger than everyone else's. When I look back on the so-called "problems" I've had in life, it's clear now why I had to go through them to get to where I am today. The next time you approach one of your problems, face it with optimism. Perhaps, the problem you are going through will teach you something. Our problems can give us a new perspective on life. Just like my dad helped me see some good in my problems, hopefully I've helped you approach your problems with a new perspective. Decide to see the five percent while everyone else only sees the ninety-five percent.

NOT ALL PROBLEMS ARE BAD

Josh Woodward

EXERCISE:

What is one problem in your life that you view as bad?

_____

_____

_____

_____

_____

_____

Is there anything good that can come from this problem?

_____

_____

_____

_____

_____

What is one practice you can introduce into your life to face your problems with more gratitude and perspective?

_____

_____

_____

_____

_____

_____

CHAPTER 6

FOCUS ON WHAT

IS IN FRONT OF YOU

Have you ever gone on a vacation with someone, and within the first day of getting there they are already talking about their return flight? Our brains are so quick to plan for the future that we often miss what is right in front of us. We can miss the gift of the present moment.

On Lewis Howes Podcast, *The School of Greatness*, Navy SEAL Chadd Wright tells a story about one of his friends who went through Navy SEAL training. He told his listeners about how one morning this friend doubted his ability to complete the training. Chadd said that once his friend spoke this thought into existence, he became powerless. His fear and inability to stay in the present moment forced him to quit the training [8]. What is so interesting about this story is that the man who quit did not quit during a specific training exercise. That would make more sense, wouldn't it? How many of us quit something, not because it is hard in the present moment, but because our minds fear it will be harder in the future?

Our fear is created in our mind and if not questioned or addressed, it can dictate our life.

Our imagination can be our best friend, but it can also be our worst enemy. It can bring us to beautiful pastures or cast us to hellish depths. Navy SEAL veteran, Chadd Wright, continued on to share another example of how our imagination can be our worst enemy. Wright shared how Navy SEAL candidates were asked to run one mile on the beach. Sounds simple, right? Once the candidates did this, they were told to run another mile. Still sounds like an activity that every trainee could complete, no? Here was the catch! They all had to keep running miles until they were told otherwise to stop [8].

Our imagination can...also be our worst enemy.

The candidates did not know whether their commander would make them run ten miles or one hundred miles. As you could imagine, the fear of the unknown mile parameters led to many of the trainees ringing the bell and quitting. However, those who conquered the exercise had an innate ability to stay in the present moment during their training. Instead of letting their minds drift to the dark depths of their imagination, they focused on the step in front of them.

American entrepreneur and author Jesse Itzler has shared a similar insight. Jesse lived with Monks for a short period of his life. While Itzler was living with the monks, he fulfilled certain duties around the monastery. One task Itzler was assigned to was washing the dishes. Upon noticing the overflowing sink with hundreds of dishes, a monk said to Jesse, "There's only the dish that's in your hand" [9].

...they focused on the step in front of them

I heard this story during my run across the country and was so inspired by it. When we stack our to-dos like a bunch of uncleaned dishes, we can become easily overwhelmed. When we focus on the task in front of us and stay present, we can utilize all of our resources to tackle that task to the best of our ability. I like to think I am great at multi-tasking but the truth is, I perform my best when I focus on one thing at a time.

I was in Marlinton, West Virginia after forty-five days of running. We were at a local restaurant in the town trying to get service to connect with family and friends. Once we got service, I called up my friend Alan. Alan and I have been friends ever since we were ten years old. We went to the same elementary school, middle school, high school, and college. I was really excited to talk to him and tell him how everything was going. When I told him we were over 500 miles into the run, he looked up the town I was in and said something like, "Dude you are so far away, you have like 2,500 miles left!" I'm picking on Alan with this story, but practically every person

I talked to focused on the number of miles I had left rather than the number I had already finished.

Personally, the 500 mile mark was a feat in itself. I hated running growing up. I was the kid in PE class who tried to fake being sick on the designated "mile day." I never did track or cross country or really any running-centric sport. Baseball was by far my favorite, and if you know anything about baseball, you know that you really don't have to run that much.

I never ran 500 miles in a year of my life and I did so in forty-four days across America. I was celebrating every achievement that came my way. Even when I surpassed 300 miles in Virginia, we celebrated at a local Krispy Kreme Donuts. Every few weeks on the run we had something to be proud of. Whether we were crossing into a new state or I had just set a new record of mileage, there was always something to be celebrated.

I adopted a day by day mindset on the run. I would handle problems as they came. I put my energy into the present rather than something far away. It was the only mindset I could afford to have out there.

When I just focused on how far I had come and what I had to do on a day-to-day basis, nothing else mattered. By doing this, I stopped myself from worrying about the figurative mountain that I had yet to climb. Something that helped me stay present across the USA came from something Nate told me. He told me how unlikely it was that I would ever come back to so many of the places I was running through. He was right. On some days, I would run through over three different towns. Many of those towns I ran through weren't anywhere near a major airport and sometimes the only way you could find them is if you were doing a cross country adventure like the one I was on.

I adopted a day by day mindset on the run.

Thinking about this on my daily runs really helped me stay present. When we fully grasp that we won't get another moment like the one we are experiencing right now, we are tempted to savor it. I struggled to savor every moment. In fact, there was a time on the transcontinental run when all I could think about was making it to the final day.

It was Day 151 and we were near Hereford, Texas. I thought it would be a good idea to start counting down the days I had left until reaching the Pacific Ocean. I calculated that it would take around sixty-seven more days of running until I was finished. So I wrote the number sixty-seven on a piece of paper and I pinned it to the RV wall. I continued to do this for only four more days. Why did I stop? I noticed that all I could think about on my daily runs was the miles and days I had left. It consumed me.

At this point of the challenge, I still had over two months of running and approximately 1,000 miles left. I don't care how much you have run in your life, when you think about running 1,000 miles it is completely overwhelming. Instead of motivating me, it did the opposite. Days 151 through 154 were incredibly difficult for me. Nate had noticed a shift in my energy ever since we started counting down the days. He crumbled up the piece of paper after Day 154 and I immediately felt a weight come off of my shoulders. Once again, I was able to focus my attention on the present moment and regain the day-to-day mindset.

Bill Belichick is one of the greatest coaches in the history of the National Football League for a reason. Watch any interview with Belichick and listen to his response when they ask him a question about the future. He only focuses on what his team is doing to get better that week. He knows that in order for his team to play their best, they need to be 100% present and can't afford to entertain distractions. As of right now, the man has six Super Bowl victories and you rarely see him crack a smile. Do I think Belichick can work on the celebrating part? Sure, but that's his choice.

Let's pretend you are training for a half marathon. Instead of constantly thinking about how you are going to run thirteen miles on race day, just think about your running goals for this week. Then, maybe when next week rolls around you can think about how many miles you want to run that week and so on and so forth. Give yourself a pat on the back as you train, and remember to keep that day-by-day mentality when it gets hard. I really don't think I would have been able to complete my cross country run if I didn't make a daily effort to stay in the present moment. While others focused on how many miles I had left, I focused on how many miles I had completed and how many I had to do on that specific day.

There were numerous days across America that I picked a rock ten yards in front of me as my target. When I reached it, I would choose another rock in the distance to get to. Don't ring the bell. If you are thinking about quitting, just take it one mile at a time, one rock at a time, and one dish at a time. You got this.

FOCUS ON WHAT IS RIGHT IN FRONT OF YOU

The troublesome calendar that was put up in the RV for motivation

EXERCISE:

Do you focus on the present moment while tackling your dreams?

_____

_____

_____

_____

_____

If so, way to go! If not, what is one thing you can do to become more present?

_____

_____

_____

_____

Why is it important to stay present when you go after your dreams?

_____

_____

_____

_____

CHAPTER 7

DON'T POSTPONE JOY

I believe there is a time to throw your hands up and celebrate and there is a time to "grind." I think both mentalities can exist together. In the last couple years, the grind and hustle culture has become very popular in our society.

While keeping your head down and grinding may help you reach your goals, it may be at the expense of enjoying the ride completely. Grinding can come with the connotation that you can't achieve your goals while enjoying yourself. Why can't you work hard and enjoy yourself at the same time? I believe you can do both.

Our lives are like a ride at an amusement park. It goes up and it goes down, but eventually it comes to an abrupt stop. You can lift your hands up in the sky and scream at the top of your lungs, or you can count the seconds until the ride ends. If you don't connect with the rollercoaster ride example, I have another analogy for you. I am full of analogies.

In soccer the objective is to strike the ball into the net. When you watch a team score a goal on tv it is an absolute spectacle. The fans lose their mind and the players might slide on the grass and sometimes take their jerseys off too. After a few minutes, the players get their composure back and the game continues. We are really good at celebrating our goals and scores. But what about celebrating the dribbles in between the goals? There is a whole journey in between achieving our dream that goes uncelebrated. If we are only focused on the big promotion, new house, new car, or other big moments, we miss all of the other special moments along the way. Is it possible to enjoy the process altogether? The practices, the scrimmages, and the games?

There is a whole journey in between achieving our dream that goes uncelebrated.

I not only think it is possible but I think it is advantageous to your quality of life. When you enjoy the process, you can appreciate all that comes with it before the season of life comes to an end. If you didn't connect to the rollercoaster or soccer example, don't worry! I have a real life example for you.

Before running across America, I ran the Los Angeles Marathon. If you've ran a marathon before, you know how hard the first one is. Leading up to the race, I had so many people tell me that it would be an experience unlike any other. And as you could imagine, I heard many people talk about the wall that runners face. "The wall" is a common phrase used in running and refers to the figurative wall that runners hit during a tough, long run.

On top of that, I heard about how thousands of supporters cheer you on all the way from the stadium to the sea. I was planning on meeting up with members from my run club but I couldn't find them and didn't want to miss the start. Just as expected, I hit "the wall" around mile sixteen but somehow I was able to keep going and finish the race. I wish I tried harder to find my friends instead of worrying about starting on time. I also wish I embraced the fans and other runners more. I remember when I crossed the finish line I expected to feel something but I didn't. It was because I didn't take in the whole experience, and told myself that my run across America would be different. I would focus more on the process and the journey, which is the most rewarding part of all.

Across America, I was heavily focused on the running component but also allowed myself to acknowledge the experience as a whole. During the journey, I left my bubble every once in a while and experienced different people and places. This balance helped me tremendously when it came to the running part. Actually, a lot of my favorite moments from the trip occurred when I wasn't running.

In DC, we ran past the White House and explored all of the monuments at night. In Nashville and Memphis, we listened to live music. In Amarillo, TX we spray-painted our names on the Cadillac Ranch. In New Mexico, we watched the sun go down at the White Sands national monument. In Tucson, AZ we attended the homecoming football game at my alma mater, The University of Arizona (BEAR DOWN ARIZONA!).

We also started traditions like going to movie theaters in every state we crossed. I am a huge movie buff, so popcorn, raisinets (Nate gave me a hard time for liking these), and a good movie was the perfect reward for a hard day's run. If we were in the middle of nowhere, we would pop *Game of Thrones* into the RV DVD player. If my kids read this one day they will probably ask, "Dad, what is a DVD?" Needless to say, we had a lot of down time so we did our best to venture out and explore.

One of our favorite experiences came in Richwood, a small town of 2,000 people in West Virginia. Jake and Nikki, a local couple, heard of our story and invited us over for breakfast. Sabine, their neighbor and our waitress from the night before (like I said, it was a small town) came over and joined. After breakfast, they showed us around their town and introduced us to all of their friends. We returned back to town the next day to watch a live concert with a local musician named Charles Godwin. After the concert, one of the firefighters named Craig let us tour his firehouse. And then the following day, my new friend Jake joined me on my run and we clocked thirteen miles together!

When Jake and Nikki invited us over for breakfast that first day, I was hesitant about joining. Like the soccer example from before, I was so focused on "scoring the goal" at that point in time. I thought that delaying my run that morning would disrupt my routine. Ironically, it became one of my favorite memories from the trip.

I almost rejected the opportunity to have breakfast with locals because of "the grind." I was so deeply attached to the routine I had, that I almost let a wonderful opportunity slip away. We can be so focused on the destination and end result of achieving our goals, that we forget to enjoy ourselves along the journey.

My cross country trip wouldn't have been the same without these incredible experiences I had outside of running. When your life is coming to a close, will you think about all the extra work you should have completed? Or, will you think about all the wonderful experiences you shared with close friends and loved ones? What will be your life's greatest moment? For me, running into the Pacific Ocean at the end of my journey was certainly sweet, but it's not my greatest moment. I love this question because it really makes us think about what is important in our lives.

My cross country trip wouldn't have been the same without these incredible experiences I had outside of running.

Perhaps your greatest life moment is related to a personal achievement, or maybe it is related to an experience you shared with a friend or loved one. Grinding and hustling to reach your goals is important, but it can be isolating. And because of that, we can miss out on beautiful shared moments. I like to think there is more to life than personally reaching our goals.

Reaching goals and personal achievements is a significant part of life, but remember that those are merely destinations. The true journey lies in the shared experiences along the way. Although we are led to believe so, personal achievements do not fill our cup in life. One of the world's best selling artists, Ed Sheeran, sings, "Success is nothing if you have no one else to share it with," in his song "The Man." Instead of being so focused on what you are doing, let's focus more on why you are doing it and especially who you are doing it for or with.

The greatest moment in my life was during my sister's speech at a Make-A-Wish event. As a teenager, my sister Katelyn was granted a wish from the non-profit Make-A-Wish when she was battling life-threatening brain cancer. I remember regularly visiting her in the hospital at a young age. Watching her tell her story on a Make-A-Wish stage over ten years later as a cancer survivor was EVERYTHING.

I didn't feel anything when I finished the LA Marathon because I was just chasing a feeling. Sound familiar? Ask yourself why you are chasing a certain goal or dream and don't hold back. Let's say you are working towards buying a "huge" house. Dissect that. Why do you want to buy this? Maybe you want others to accept you and you think buying a mansion will do that. Keep dissecting! Why do you want others to accept you so much? Perhaps you aren't accepted because you don't have a lot of money, and once you have a nice big house, this will change. "Once I have that house everything will change," you say to yourself. Statements like "Once I do this," or, "When I get that," and "One day when," are destination focused phrases. I am all for people setting big goals, just don't do it simply for the feeling at the end of reaching your goal, because I can tell you that this feeling is fleeting. If you are constantly thinking about your destination, how can you find joy in the present moment?

...I was just chasing a feeling.

Each time I have chased the feeling you get after you reach a milestone, I have come up short. Instead of waiting to feel a certain way in the future, why not try to feel that way today? I learned this very simple but valuable lesson on Day 77 in Kentucky at a roadside hotdog stand. We drove past the shop but Nate suggested we turn around and check it out, and I am so thankful we did. The shop was called Paradise Point Marketplace, and we quickly became friends with the owners, Sebrina and John. John told us how he used to be a chiropractor and always dreamed of one day opening his own hot dog shop. I could see the pride on his face as he shared this story with me. John transformed his "one day" dream into day one when he opened Paradise Point with Sebrina in April of 2005. John told us that they didn't sell hot dogs or gifts at their shop, but they sold joy.

...they sold Joy.

Before we left their shop I snapped a picture of a sign outside their front door that said, "DON'T POSTPONE JOY." A simple but profound statement. A statement that goes against the current pulse of our generation to only celebrate big wins. We can all access joy right now. We don't need to wait to score the goal in order to take off our jersey and slide. We can throw our hands up in the air right now. We can celebrate all of the ups and all of the downs. While we are on the ride, we can enjoy ourselves and each other.

DON'T POSTPONE JOY

Picture taken from Paradise Point Marketplace in Kentucky

Nate and Brady meeting Sebrina and John,

owners of Paradise Point Marketplace

Brady, Nate, Sabine, Jake, and Nikki enjoying breakfast together in West Virginia

Brady dressing up as Forrest Gump on Halloween during his USA run

EXERCISE:

Do you enjoy the process of following your dream?

_____

_____

_____

_____

_____

If you don't, could it mean you are focusing too much on the outcome? How can you avoid this?

_____

_____

_____

_____

_____

_____

What is one way you can give yourself a pat on the back and celebrate the journey of following your dream?

_____

_____

_____

_____

_____

_____

CHAPTER 8

WE CAN DOUBT OURSELVES

AND STILL DO IT

J ust three days into my run across America, I started to have doubts. I was in Englishtown, New Jersey and only twenty miles into my 3,311 mile run. I woke up feeling groggy and sore. I thought to myself, "If my body is feeling this way already, how am I going to last even a month?"

How am I going to last even a month?

We went into a nearby restaurant called Luchentos Kitchen, and the waitress Janis instantly lifted our spirits. We told her our story and she paid for our meal. The start of the morning had been blue but this encounter with Janis gave me newfound hope. I went back to the RV and my perspective had shifted. I realized that every new moment on this journey was a fresh start- anything could happen.

I knew I could turn it around and have a positive run despite my early morning doubts. I put my doubt and discouraged feelings aside for a moment, and became curious. "What if I could still put my shoes on?" I thought to myself. If I could put my shoes on, I could go one mile. And if I could run one mile I could go another and another.

I was able to put a great run together that day. This experience showed me that I could doubt myself and not "feel great" but still get it done. As long as I kept moving, my doubts could not stop me. Time after time on my run, I doubted myself, detached myself from those feelings, and focused on what I could do. Eventually, I stopped paying credence to every doubt that arose.

I got my running routine down to a science. Every morning after I woke up, I got my workout outfit on, ate breakfast, rolled my yoga mat out, started stretching, arranged my water pack, left the RV and started moving. It didn't matter what doubts consumed my mind earlier in the morning. If I could make it out of the RV and start moving, I would set myself up for success that day. The last few months of the run, I even started sleeping in my workout clothes to jumpstart my routine. Dressing before a run was one less thing I had to think about.

When I was ninety-one days into my run, I conditioned myself to believe that I could put in work, regardless of my mental or physical condition. I was in Linden, Tennessee and was fighting a bad cold I had picked up days before in Nashville. It was day six of running with congestion and a runny nose. Instead of sleeping it off, I decided to run through it. I found myself drinking DayQuil right before some of the runs, and kept Kleenex in my running pack. On Day 92, I wrapped up seven straight days of running through a bad cold. Ironically, I ran one of my farthest weeks in distance for a total of 120 miles.

A lot of our thoughts and fears come from a place of self-preservation. And in some cases those thoughts are necessary, but in others they hold us back. Extreme ultra endurance athlete Colin O'Brady has shared how doubts are a struggle in his life. Despite crossing Antarctica solo, summiting Mt. Everest twice, and rowing from South America to Antarctica, he still experiences doubt.

O'Brady coins his experience of all time highs in life as "tens" on a scale of "one to ten." He talks about how his low moments, or ones, were necessary to reach his tens. He shares how most people don't want to experience anything too low or too high in life. They would rather stay between four to six, the zone of "comfortable complacency" [10]. This common comfort zone that Colin describes could be the result of doubts controlling us.

TEDx speaker Trevor Ragan describes this process beautifully in his talk about overcoming fear and doubt. He talks about something called the "lizard brain." In slang, the limbic system is referred to as the lizard brain because the limbic system is about all a lizard has for brain function. This part of our brain determines if something is safe or dangerous. If we perceive something as uncomfortable or dangerous, our brain will signal distress and fears or doubts will pop up. This can be beneficial when we come across serious threats. But like Ragan hinted to, our world is becoming more and more accustomed to living in a state of comfort. This means our lizard brain is constantly steering us away from anything that could pose discomfort in our lives.

Ragan gives an example of how it is much easier for him to drive to Chipotle as opposed to taking the time to shop for food and cook a healthy meal. Ragan explains how we should think of the lizard brain as a backseat driver. While your fears and doubts will try to give you directions, *you* ultimately decide where the car will drive [11].

If I titled the second edition of this book *How to Get Rid of Fear*, it would be flying off of the shelves. Everyone wishes they could fearlessly live life. The title of Ragan's TEDx Talk, *How to 'overcome' fear itself*, is so profound in itself. At a quick glance, someone might click on his video because they want to get rid of fear altogether. I believe Trevor emphasizes "overcome" in his title because it's impossible to overcome fear. I agree with Trevor. Fear is with us. You may overcome it, but it can always show up again around the corner. If fear will always be a part of our life experience, what can we do about it? I believe we can fight fear and doubt with curiosity. We can ask ourselves what is on the other side of our doubts and fears. Could our doubts and fears be rightfully protecting us? Sure! But what if a certain doubt or fear is holding you back from following your destiny? Let's talk about the universal language and something we can all understand, love.

English poet Alfred Lord Tennyson once said, "'Tis better to have loved and lost than never to have loved at all." Have you found yourself in love or close to it at least once in your life? While love can feel like you are on top of a mountain, it can also feel like you are burning alive in hot lava, or so I've heard (winky face). To put it simply, love comes with its risks. Doubts and fears can lead some of us to not experience love entirely. The fear that love can hurt us cripples us. The potential downfall of love can overshadow all it has to offer. It is more safe for us to choose the option where we guarantee we won't get hurt. The lizard brain could win in this situation, too.

I believe we can fight fear and doubt with curiosity.

One of my favorite films is *Goodwill Hunting* with the legendary actor Robin Williams. There is a scene where Williams' character, Sean Maguire, is consoling a young, confused and lost boy named Will Hunting. Maguire teaches Will about love. He shares a personal story about the love of his life. He explains how he lost his wife Susan to cancer and despite the tragic loss and pain, he didn't regret one moment he spent with her, even in her final days. Sean hits Will with this famous line, *"You don't know about real loss, 'cause it only occurs when you've loved something more than you love yourself. And I doubt you've ever dared to love anybody that much."* It is an emotional exchange and a very touching part of the film. The phrase that jumps out to me in this famous scene is, "dared to love." It takes daring action to love despite all of our most daunting doubts and fears. Love takes courage. Heck, life itself takes courage. Courage is a necessary skill for us to push past our fears and doubts. Courage helps us storm past the lizard brains default mode for comfort.

Colin O' Brady warns us that our doubts can lead to living in the "zone of comfortable complacency." Trevor Ragan encourages us to think of the "lizard brain" as a backseat driver. Robin Williams' character Sean explains how courage is needed to overcome our greatest fears and doubts. We can dare to love. We can silence our lizard brain. We can experience the peak moments and climb life's greatest mountains. We can get to our destination with or without that backseat driver. Finally, we can and we must lace up our shoes on days we feel hopeless.

WE CAN DOUBT OURSELVES AND STILL DO IT

Nate, Janis (Middle), and Brady on day three of Brady's run across America

EXERCISE:

What is one doubt that has been popping up recently relating to your goals?

_____

_____

_____

_____

_____

_____

Will you allow your doubts and fears to control you?

_____

_____

_____

_____

What could be on the other side of these doubts and fears? What would it feel like to conquer these doubts and fears?

_____

_____

_____

_____

CHAPTER 9

WE CAN'T DO IT ALONE

Bestselling Author and International Speaker, Simon Sinek, shares the importance of the last step of Alcoholics Anonymous (AA). Sinek points out that the individuals who are able to do the last step are much more likely to stay sober. The last step involves helping others overcome alcoholism [12]. We need each other. Many of us try to overcome every single obstacle in our lives without any outside help. I believe it is not only okay to accept help from others, but healthy to ask for help.

When your schedule is packed and someone offers to help you with something, do you accept their help? Or do you try to do everything on your own? When my sister Katelyn was fighting brain cancer at the age of sixteen, my parents were pretty overwhelmed as you could imagine. When we are completely overwhelmed with life, even the most ordinary tasks can feel grueling. I remember local parents and family friends stopping by our house with cooked meals for our family. My parents acted as if they could handle putting dinner on the table despite the circumstances, but deep down I knew they needed help. Fortunately, my parents put their pride aside and welcomed the support.

Being eight years old at the time, many people were looking out for me, too. One time, a teacher at my elementary school took me to a local toy store after school. Additionally, a school psychologist pulled me out of class regularly to make sure I was okay. My parents didn't know about this until years later. I am forever grateful for all of the kind people who helped our family during that difficult time. We couldn't have made it through that ordeal alone. We didn't overcome it on our own, it was a team effort.

Towards the end of 2018 and the start of 2019, I was at one of the lowest points in my life. I was wasting my days away with alcohol and sleep. I questioned my purpose in life at every turn. Many mornings I would wake up full of sadness. I felt numb inside and I dreaded waking up every single day. The depression was heavy and felt like a weighted blanket sucking me into my sorrow. When I first experienced depression, I was in college and relied on my faith and family to get me through it. This time I was living in LA, not practicing my faith, and I was trying to get through it all by myself (and Jack Daniels).

On the first day of 2019, I made a new friend named Jacyn. Jacyn was a bit older than me but we connected right away. She was a great listener and an incredibly accepting person. It turned out that she was a practicing life coach! A few months passed since meeting her and I really needed someone to talk to, but I was scared to reach out to her. I finally found the courage to call her, and not only did she listen, but she showed me that it was okay for me to not be okay.

Whether she knew it or not, my life was forever changed. The following day, I rolled over in my bed and wrote the idea to run across America in my journal.

We all can find the courage to shine our light when others grant us the space to fully be ourselves. But the key here is, it takes the people around us to inspire courage - to light the flame within. Every single one of you reading or hearing this has a figurative flame inside of you. But just like lighting a candle, a flame has to be ignited. You can try to ignite it on your own, or you can let someone else ignite it for you. In my life experience, my flame has burned the brightest when I've allowed others to inspire and help me. When I resisted help and tried to do life alone, my flame withered.

Just as plants survive on sunlight, I survive and thrive on inspiration. Inspiration can come from anything: a sunset, a song, a movie, or even a quote. One of my favorite quotes comes from Marianne Williamson in a movie called *Coach Carter*.

...My flame has burned the brightest when I've allowed others to inspire and help me.

The quote is recited by one of the basketball players named Timo. For context, Timo and his basketball team were going through a difficult time. While their team was performing on the court, they were failing in the classroom. Timo and the rest of his teammates were suspended for their academic performance by the team coach, Mr. Carter. In an act of leadership, Timo stands up and recites Williamson's quote.

It is an extensive quote, but I will share the piece of it that has helped ignite a flame within me during the lowest times in my life. It goes like this, "We are all meant to shine as children do. It is not just in some of us, it is in everyone. And as we let our own light shine, we unconsciously give other people the permission to do the same." Like an olympic runner passing the torch on to someone else, I believe that this quote serves as a similar anecdote. When we find the courage inside to shine our light, it automatically inspires someone else to follow suit, or to grab the torch and run with it. Life is a relay and the torch cannot be passed on alone. In order for a blaze to spread like wildfire, it needs fuel. We are that fuel. We need each other.

I received so much fuel on my journey across the USA. Charles Wesley Godwin told me to crawl if I had to, and do whatever it takes. Super Bowl MVP, Ray Lewis, sent me a personal video on my birthday saying, "You are a light in this world, Brady." A mystery truck driver left me a bag of trail mix near the highway call box labeled, "long distance runner!" A fan named Wilma sent me a pink bracelet with the word "hope" all over it. A bartender named Guy and a lovely waitress named Gloria who served us in New Jersey consistently checked in and donated to our cause. I received daily texts and videos from Luke and my run club. I had countless facetimes with family and friends. The list goes on and on. Our fuel source across America was not just food. It was family, friends, and fellowship.

We need each other.

As I mention in Chapter Four, the closest time my flame came to running out was during my achilles scare. I was so close to hanging up my running shoes when that happened. While I felt like I was sinking in quicksand, the natural thing for me to do was to put my hand out and reach for help. I needed some fuel in the form of support and inspiration.

I vulnerably posted about what I was going through on my Instagram and referenced my dad's advice to take it easy. The Grammy nominated musician Mike Posner commented "ur dad is right." When Posner tells you to listen to your dad, you do it. Mike was also walking across America at the time so we would encourage each other back and forth, and his words during this time really gave me hope. His support reminded me of Jacyn's encouragement and again made me feel like it was okay to not be okay.

I received endless amounts of supportive messages during this time. There was one message that I'll never forget. The message came from one of my supporters, Charlotte Musgrove. She said, "Lean on this army of a support team you have and let that carry you till you've built your strength back." Just like Jacyn and Mike let me know it was okay to not be okay, Charlotte's words reminded me that I wasn't alone.

Before making it to San Diego to finish my transcontinental run, I set an arrival date for friends and family to join me. My family helped organize an incredible celebration for the final day. The shirt design they sent me was incredible but it had one major flaw. It said, "You did it!" I called my family and told them they needed to change the words on the shirt to, "We did it!" Because we truly did. It was always a team effort.

Throughout the entire journey across the USA, I rejected and ran further and further away from God. Nate would always encourage me to come pray with him at the many churches we visited or parked at, but I would stay inside the RV. Just because I rejected God, doesn't mean that God rejected me. On the final day, hundreds of people including friends and news reporters started to show up outside our RV.

With my final moments of privacy in the RV, I went through my daily gratitude practice. I reflected on everything and everyone I was grateful for. As I thought of a few blessings, something happened that was completely unexpected. A tsunami of love came streaming down my face. I cried harder than I ever had in my life that morning. In that moment, I was overflowing with gratitude.

Recently, I heard my friend Frank Shirley say something that perfectly described this feeling. Frank heard a minister at a funeral service once say, "Tears are prayers that we couldn't put into words." Everything I had gone through in my life and everyone who had been a part of my journey was no coincidence. I felt complete reassurance that everything I had experienced in my life was a part of a plan, God's plan. God was with me every step of the journey across the USA and throughout my life.

I was overflowing with gratitude.

Someone out there is ready to listen. Turning to God has always brought me immense peace, grace, hope and strength. If that doesn't work for you, the Jacyn's, Mike's, and Charlotte's of the world can also ignite your flame. You just have to look for them.

If we don't ask for help when we need it, how can we be of help to others? If you need someone to talk to, please don't be afraid to ask for help. There is true freedom in making this decision. I have one favor to ask of you. One day when you are stronger and your flame is burning bright, please pass the torch on to someone else!

WE CAN'T DO IT ALONE

A kind stranger left Brady a bag of trail mix at a callbox in California

Brady meeting one of his supporters Wilma in Oklahoma

Brady's friends and family celebrating with him on the beach following his historic cross country run

EXERCISE:

Who is one person that has been there for you in times of need?
What did they do?

_____

_____

_____

_____

_____

_____

_____

What is one way you can acknowledge and thank them for what they
have done for you? Do it.

_____

_____

_____

_____

_____

_____

_____

_____

Extra Credit: Think of one person you can support today. Show up for them in the simplest of ways!

_____

_____

_____

_____

_____

_____

_____

CHAPTER 10

WE CAN ALWAYS GIVE A LITTLE MORE

Throughout my USA run, I was consistently perplexed to learn that we can always give a little more. The key word here is always. I was reminded of this lesson recently, which urged me to revisit the original publication of this book. I knew I could give a little bit more and even if it was one extra sentence, I wanted to add more value to this work.

I want to share a human experiment I heard of years ago. A group of people were asked to close their eyes and reach their hands as high as they can go. Then, they were told to open their eyes and raise their hands even higher, and they did just that! What is so interesting about this experiment is that the initial instruction was for everyone to raise their hands as high as they could. Based on that point, wouldn't it make sense for everyone's hands to stay exactly where they were the second time around? When we are pushed to our limits, we can raise our hands even higher and give a little more.

I put this experiment to the test during a presentation in business school and like I hoped for, everyone raised their hands higher. It was risky to test this out with my grade on the line, but it worked out. If you don't trust this experiment, try it out on your family or group of friends later - just make sure they haven't read this book yet.

Have you ever been to a group fitness class where the instructor singles you out during the workout? If so, you know how embarrassing this could be. When I know someone is keeping their eye on me, I will put in more effort. Call it competition or accountability, but the point is that I can always give a little bit more in every situation. Why is it that we don't give 100% when we are asked for it? This is a complicated question. We could be sick, tired, anxious and overall feeling like crap, but we can still give a little more than our best.

I can't count the number of days I learned this lesson across the USA. Regardless if I was unwell, injured, or mentally weak, as long as I laced up my shoes and got out the RV door, I was always able to go the extra mile (figuratively and literally). I often sent Nate a pickup location to meet me at when the day's run came to an end. There he would be, parked on the side of the road. All I had to do was aim for the RV where a shower and comfortable bed awaited me. A lot of the time, I ran right by the RV and yelled something like, "I got one more, I got one more!" Eventually, I stayed silent and gestured to Nate how many miles I had left.

When my body and mind first showed me I could go further despite terrible conditions, it was hard to comprehend. Then, it became expected. I knew that no matter how bad I felt physically and mentally, I could always run a little bit longer. Let's look at a few examples of humans doing extraordinary things under unfavorable circumstances. Our first example of this takes us to Okinawa, Japan during World War II.

431 men were awarded the United States Medal of Honor out of a whopping sixteen million active soldiers. Out of those men to receive the nation's greatest honor was Desmond Doss. What is so special about this man? He served in the war without firing a single bullet. He actually didn't even carry a weapon at battle. His sole purpose was to save lives instead of taking lives. He carried the Bible with him as he heroically charged towards injured men crying out, "Medic!" Doss is most recognized for what happened at Hacksaw Ridge.

Shortly after American soldiers overtook the ridge, the enemy forces caused them to retreat. Desmond Doss disobeyed the orders given to him and refused to retreat down the ridge with his fellow soldiers. Instead, he stayed in the fight and ran to injured soldiers in need of help without a weapon to defend himself. He is believed to have rescued at least 75 men on Hacksaw Ridge that night. Desmond was interviewed later in his life about this experience and shared how he prayed, "God, give me one more." Desmond found something deep inside himself and did more than was humanly possible. When President Truman awarded Doss the Medal of Honor he said, "I consider this a greater honor than being the President" [13].

Many times, athletes have shocked the world by giving more of themselves during the gloomiest of times. The first magnificent story happened in my hometown of San Diego back in 2008. Tiger Woods won the US Open, one of the world's biggest golf tournaments, in comeback fashion. His victory and scorecard was impressive but that is not what made the headlines or what made the victory memorable.

Woods confirmed two days after the tournament that he had been playing with two stress fractures in his leg and a torn ACL. Just playing with one of these injuries would come with insurmountable pain. If you've never seen it, go back and watch the highlights from the tournament. You will see Tiger limping and grimacing almost entirely throughout the tournament. At one point, he uses his golf club as a cane just to hold his body up [14]. Woods' caddy warned Tiger that playing through this injury could end his career, and in a defiant response Tiger said, "I am going to win this tournament" [15]. This is a perfect example of someone who was able to give a little more under the most unfavorable physical conditions.

If you are a basketball fan, you probably know where I am going next. The one and only, Michael Jordan, is highly regarded as the greatest basketball player of all time. Among all of Jordan's astonishing accolades, there is one specific game of his that supports this idea of giving a little bit more. This game is referred to as the "Flu Game" [16]. It was game five of the NBA finals and Jordan's team, the Chicago Bulls, was playing the Utah Jazz.

The series was tied 2-2, and whoever won the game would be just one game away from an NBA Championship title. Jordan was playing with "food poisoning or a sudden and severe virus." Jordan looked completely out of it on the court, but somehow he was able to give a little bit more. That little bit more added up to MJ scoring thirty-eight points, including a clutch three point shot in the last half minute, leading to the Bulls' victory.

In a postgame interview, Jordan said, "I was really tired, I was very weak. Somehow, I found the energy. Just stayed strong, I wanted it really bad." Similar to Woods, MJ found something inside of him to push harder despite the circumstances weighing him down.

Our final sports moment comes from the baseball diamond. I played baseball for thirteen years when I was younger and learned a lot about life from the sport. One of the most powerful lessons I learned is that you need a strong approach at the plate. When you step up to the plate, your thoughts matter. If I was thinking to myself, "Don't strikeout, Brady," the battle was already lost. One of the most memorable moments in the sport of professional baseball came from a man with a fearless approach at the plate. When the rest of the world didn't think he stood a chance, he knew he could give a little more for his team and the city of Los Angeles.

The year was 1988 and the Los Angeles Dodgers were down by one run. They were one out away from losing the first game of the World Series against the Oakland Athletics. One of the Dodgers best hitters Kirk Gibson was unable to play in the game because of an injured left hamstring and swollen right knee [17]. In baseball, one could argue that your legs and hips are just as valuable for swinging the bat than your upper body. Gibson cornered Coach Tommy Lasorda and begged him to be put into the game. To make this real life movie script even better, the Dodgers substituted Gibson into the ninth inning of the game with everything on the line.

Gibson limped on both legs as he walked to the batter's box. There was one man on base so if Gibson could miraculously hit a home run, the Dodgers would win the game. One foul ball after the other, Gibson was unable to put much pressure on either of his legs. He hopped from one leg to the other, as if he was walking on hot potatoes.

Gibson stood in the box with a defiant approach. He wasn't going down without a fight. He was trying to give a little bit more than he could possibly give. The count was three balls and two strikes. On the eighth pitch at bat, A's pitcher Dennis Eckersley let go of the ball and Gibson's bat connected. Eckersley stood in awe. The ball soared to the right field bleachers of Dodgers stadium, and the Dodgers won the game! Gibson pulled off the impossible. He limped around the bases pumping his fist into the air, and history was made.

Gibson, MJ, Woods, and Doss were all able to find something deep down inside themselves to push further when everyone else counted them out. All of them were able to give a little bit more and shock the world. Speaking of shocking... Do you know the story of how electricity came to be? Even if you do, a reminder of this can still spark something inside of you.

The reason there is light in this coffee shop I am typing in right now is because of a man named Thomas Edison - I am sure you have heard of him! Mr. Edison is famous for creating the light bulb of course, but many details leading to this world-changing invention go unmentioned.

According to the Edison Innovation Foundation, Edison attempted to spark electricity over 10,000 times. When interviewed about this process, Edison said, "I have not failed. I have just found 10,000 ways that don't work."

We often claim that people like Thomas Edison are geniuses or talents that can't be reproduced. Edison also said, "Genius is one percent inspiration, ninety-nine percent perspiration." I believe that Edison would not consider himself a genius if he were here today, but instead someone who always gave a little bit more. "Our greatest weakness lies in giving up. The most certain way to succeed is always to try just one more time," said Edison [18]. This insight should encourage us all! If something as monumental as electricity can be created by nonstop persistence and perspiration, we all are capable of greatness. Greatness is in our control. We can choose to keep going and we can choose to give a little more.

This lesson of giving a little more, like every other one, can be applied to any facet of your life. Studying for a test, trying to get that promotion at work, wanting to be a better parent, etc. When our backs are up against the wall and it feels like we have nothing left, we can always give a little bit more. We all can raise our hands higher.

We all can run past Nate and the RV. We all can be like Desmond Doss and run towards danger while everyone else is retreating. We all can swing through the pain like Tiger. When the temperature is high, we all can drain the shot like MJ. We all can limp to the plate like Gibson. And when darkness surrounds us like Edison, we all can keep trying to find the spark!

WE CAN ALWAYS GIVE A LITTLE MORE

Brady pictured at the Texas border on Day 142

Brady taking in a moment of prayer after crossing
into his home state, California, on Day 202

EXERCISE:

I want you to take a hard look at yourself in the mirror. Can you give
more than you are currently giving towards your dream life?

_____

_____

_____

_____

_____

_____

If you answered yes, you are on the right path. We can all give a little more! Acknowledging this is a start. Now, think of what you can do to add more to your life. It can be small! Write it down.

_____

_____

_____

_____

_____

_____

CHAPTER 11

BELIEVE IN WHAT YOU CAN'T SEE

I t was game four of the 2004 MLB American League Championship. It had been eighty-six years since the Red Sox had won a championship. Everyone and their mother thought the New York Yankees would defeat the Boston Red Sox and move on to the World Series. The white board in the Red Sox locker room read, "We can change history! Believe it!" Prior to game four, one of the more cheerful players on the Red Sox, Kevin Millar, was interviewed. He told the reporter, "Don't let us win today. We got Pedy tomorrow, we got Shill game six. And game seven, anything can happen!"

No team in MLB history had ever come back from down three games to zero in a seven game series - But Millar and his team saw a path. They believed in something that no one else could see. The Red Sox won the next four games making MLB history and ending the "curse" [19].

At times, our imagination can work against us. But, our imagination can help us if used the right way. There is power in believing in something you can't yet see. Our imagination can be used for good. Our imagination can give us the roadmap to where we are headed.

Even though we will fall off course from time to time, this vision paves a way for us to get back on track. It serves as our hope. When storms shake us and our compass is broken, our vision can help us see the rainbow on the horizon.

I want you to look around for a second. Perhaps you see restaurants, gas stations, highways, office buildings, retail shops, and more. Most of what you see everyday did not just appear out of thin air - it came to life from a vision. Someone thought to themselves, "I wonder what this will look like someday." My dad is a very accomplished developer, and the founder of Affirmed Housing, a company that produces affordable housing in all of California. When I was a kid, my dad would take me to his projects in downtown, San Diego. One project my dad took me to stands out among the rest. The project was called Ten Fifty B, and when he first took me on the site there was nothing to see but a huge pit that was excavated below me.

My dad told me this pit would eventually become a twenty-three story giant apartment complex - it was hard to believe. While I could only see a giant pit of dirt, my dad had a vision. Months later, when the mayor of San Diego and many others celebrated Ten Fifty B's grand opening, I remembered that pit of dirt. My dad turned a pit of dirt into something extraordinary. He brought his vision to life. My dad shared with me that the technical verbiage for this process is called "concept drawing."

...Our vision can help us see the rainbow on the horizon.

Many people who bring their dreams to life first draw it out and get it down on paper. I've already touched on the hardships that the wildly successful actor and comedian Jim Carrey endured throughout his life. Carrey in fact was a big believer in this. While Carrey was a struggling actor and in his own "pit of dirt," he did two very unusual things.

During an interview with Oprah Winfrey, he said he wrote himself a check. The check was for ten million dollars. Carrey dated the check Thanksgiving 1995. He shared with Winfrey how he kept it in his wallet and said it deteriorated and deteriorated for years. Then, Carrey shared that just before Thanksgiving of 1995, he received a check for ten million dollars for his acting services in the hit movie, *Dumb and Dumber*. Carrey also shared with Winfrey that he would routinely drive up Mulholland Drive - where many celebrities and actors lived. Carrey was poor at the time, but imagined one day being a successful actor whom directors wanted to work with [20]. What once was a pit of dirt to Jim Carrey was dirt no more.

Sometimes picturing a bigger than life dream takes crazy faith. Someone who knows all about crazy faith is Michael Todd, the Pastor and leader of Transformation Church in Tulsa, Oklahoma.

When Pastor Todd's church only had 300 members back in 2015, he had a big dream that a lot of people would have called crazy. In his daughter's room, he wrote down this dream on a piece of paper. The dream was to one day purchase the fifty million dollar Spirit Center Arena in Tulsa, Oklahoma.

As the years passed, Pastor Todd visited the arena multiple times and took videos claiming that this dream would come true someday. When Pastor Todd told his real estate advisor of his aspiration to buy the Spirit Center, the advisor doubted this. Because Pastor Todd was so faithful about his dream, his real estate advisor called the arena every week to see if it was available for purchase. Years went on and still, Pastor Todd did not hear from the Spirit Center. Then, all of a sudden, an investment group from Texas was nearing an acquisition of the arena. Hours away from buying the Spirit Center, their funding fell through.

After years of prayer, Todd's real estate advisor called him and told him there was an opportunity to purchase the venue. Todd and his team didn't hesitate and seized the opportunity. The Texas group heard that Transformation Church was going to steal the deal, so they offered Pastor Todd one million dollars to back out. Todd turned down the offer. The group then came back and offered Pastor Todd one million dollars and five years of free church services in the building. He again turned down the offer. Finally, the group offered Pastor Todd two million dollars to back out of the deal.

Pastor Todd rejected the offer and because of his crazy faith, is the rightful owner of the Spirit Center today. Pastor Todd celebrated the acquisition with his church by blasting DJ Khaled's song "I Got The Keys!" over the speaker [21]. Pastor Todd turned a dream in his daughter's bedroom into an arena full of dreams. Do you see the power of writing your dreams down?

Many of you are probably familiar with the book and movie, *The Secret*. If not, it is a wonderful deep dive into the world of manifestation and visualization. It includes many accounts from people who have found success with visualization and manifestation.

One of the stories comes from a man named John Assaraf. In his younger adult years, Assaraf created vision boards for his life. Five years passed, and his vision boards were placed amongst old boxes in storage. When Assaraf's son Keenan found the boxes and the vision boards, he brought them to his father. Assaraf looked at the board in complete shock and amazement. The house he had pinned on the board five years prior was the exact house that he was living in and renovating [22]. Mr. Assaraf believed in what he couldn't see until one day it came to life before him.

Before running across the country, I needed to dream bigger than the pit I was drowning in. There were three instances in which I used visualization before and during my journey across the USA. I already mentioned earlier in this book how I wrote down the idea to run across the country in a journal around March of 2019. I wish I could find the journal but it got misplaced after moving. Similar to Assaraf,

I wrote it down and didn't look at it again. I don't know how to explain it but, it felt valuable to write it down - it empowered me.

I completely forgot about the second time I visualized my dream until I sat down to write this chapter. Days before flying to the east coast to start my run, I went to the exact beach in San Diego where I believed I would finish my journey many months later. I breathed in the fresh salty air. I imagined what it would be like to have friends and family cheer for me as I finished my historic run.

...It felt valuable to write it down.

Another time I used visualization during my running journey was while I trained for my first half marathon. I would run on the treadmill to train and I would do something very strange. I'd imagine myself crossing the finish line of the race and picture how I would celebrate in that finishing moment. I visualized that I would put my arms out to my sides as if I was running through finish line tape like an olympic runner. So that is what I did. I would close my eyes on the treadmill for a split second and put my arms to the side, and imagine myself crossing that finish line.

As I trained for my first full marathon, I practiced this same thing. And when I trained for the run across America, I put my arms to my side and did it again. Since it took 218 days to run across the country, I practiced this pose on extra tough days to remind myself of my vision. It wasn't until recently when I had an epiphany about all of this. The cover photo we chose for my first book was me standing on the beach of San Diego. Guess what I was doing with my arms in this celebratory photo? My arms were out to my sides. The finish line moment came true.

The finish line moment came true.

What was once a pit of dirt for the Boston Red Sox, became the best Cinderella story in sports history. What was once a pit of dirt for my dad turned into a beautiful twenty-three story apartment complex. What was once a pit of dirt for Jim Carrey turned into a blossoming acting career. What was once a pit of dirt for Pastor Todd transformed into the Spirit Center. What was once a pit of dirt for John Assaraf turned into the house of his dreams. What was once a pit of dirt for me turned into an ocean of possibilities.

BELIEVE IN WHAT YOU CAN'T SEE

Brady celebrating after finishing his 3,311 mile run across USA

Jim Silverwood (Brady's Dad) photographed holding project plans to one of his first developments

EXERCISE:

What will your pit of dirt turn into?

_____

_____

_____

What is one way you can visualize this? You can do this in many ways, do what feels right for you!

_____

_____

_____

_____

_____

_____

CHAPTER 12

CHOOSE PROGRESS OVER PERFECTION

A man recently told me that his son in law was a "work in progress." I thought it was a pretty funny statement. Aren't all of us a work in progress? If perfection is unattainable, isn't the next best thing progress? Winston Churchill once said that, "Perfection is the enemy of progress."

When we become overly obsessed with our goals, we can lose perspective. If you are an artist, you know exactly what I am talking about. The average person at an art gallery may stop at a piece of art that catches their eye. But after some time, they will keep walking around and look at other paintings.

When we become overly obsessed with our goals, we can lose perspective.

If you are an artist of the work, you might stare at your work for hours and hours and hours. You may inspect it and zoom in on every blemish that exists within the work. It may discourage you so much that you stop working on the piece or you hide it from the world. We can do the same thing with our dreams and goals. If we zoom in too closely, we can miss the big picture entirely and throw away the masterpiece - our dream.

Where are all my perfectionists at? I get it. When I set goals for myself, I get very attached to them and when I don't reach said goals, my perfectionist side comes out. I am my toughest critic. And I do not hold back! It has always been me versus myself. I scold myself and wonder if I can try to fix the outcome somehow. Because of this, there have been many times I missed the big picture entirely. Goals are great, but they are not everything! Whether we hit our goals or not, they do not define who we are or how we are doing.

Imagine your New Year's resolution is to lose twenty pounds. If you lost two pounds every month you would be on pace to lose over twenty pounds in a year. After the first month, you check the scale and instead of losing two pounds, you realize you gained two pounds. You decide to give up on the New Year's resolution. In this case, I would tell you that you are missing the point entirely. What are the reasons behind your goal? Maybe it is to be healthier or more disciplined. Perhaps you still can achieve those things. Progress and movement towards your goals is movement nonetheless. Confucius says, "It does not matter how slow you go as long as you don't stop." If you give it your full effort and fall short of your goals, give yourself a pat on the back. Sometimes in life, it is just not your day.

__Progress and movement towards your goals is movement nonetheless.__

When I started my run across the country, I set a micro goal that I would not walk a single mile. To whoever is reading this, that may sound like a silly goal but to me it meant a lot. Every mile I trekked on foot would be run and not walked. I was able to do this for about forty days until West Virginia. West Virginia had some San Francisco steep hills. The incline mixed with the intense summer humidity, left me no choice but to walk. When I chose to walk for a couple minutes that day I felt ashamed and disappointed in myself. Then, I meditated on it and realized that it was completely okay to have evolving goals. My big goal was to run across the country but the even bigger, overarching goal was to inspire myself and others while raising money for charity. I was accomplishing that big picture goal every day, whether I was running the whole time or not.

One more day that sticks out to me is Day 193 in Arizona. By this time on the run, I was running twenty miles daily pretty easily. But, on the 193rd day, I could not run for my life. I was on the struggle bus. I ran eleven miles and called it quits. I remember just shrugging my shoulders and knowing there wasn't anything else I could do. The next day, I got back to my twenty mile self and I was back on track. Sometimes, we have an off day and we just need to shrug our shoulders. And like Taylor Swift's hit song, sometimes we just have to, "shake it off" and keep moving forward. Why? Because every step forward is one more step closer to our dream.

When I think about perfection, I think about how it is an impossible target to hit. For us at least! The only human I can think of that has lived a perfect life was Jesus. And no one can be Jesus but Jesus himself. While you can't be Jesus, you can pretend to be him on TV! Perhaps you have watched the hit show called, *The Chosen*. In the docuseries, *Jonathan and Jesus*, Jonathan Roumie reveals what it is like playing such a monumental figure - Jesus. Jonathan shares how he constantly deals with the struggle of trying to be like Jesus and falling short.

Because so many people feel the love of Jesus through Jonathan's acting, he feels even more pressure to be like Jesus in public. I cannot even begin to fathom how much pressure a situation like that could be for a person. However, Jonathan strikes me as someone who has relied on progress over perfection in his career. He shares in the documentary that a mentor of his once told him it could take him twenty years to reach success in his acting career. Sure enough, it took over twenty years for Jonathan to land his first big TV role for *The Chosen*, which is now one of the biggest shows in the world. Just weeks prior to landing the role, Roumie was running out of money. Imagine how many times in those twenty years and especially the days leading up to *The Chosen*, that Jonathan thought about quitting [23]. But he didn't quit. He kept putting in the work year after year. He valued progress over perfection.

I recently gave my first TEDx talk at the University of Purdue. Giving a TEDx talk was a dream of mine for over four years. In 2020, I looked into it and tried to look up some information about events but nothing really materialized. I revisited this dream in 2023 after three years of no movement. I contacted an old friend from high school, Jake Heibrunn, who I knew had given a talk on the TEDx stage. Jake connected me with a program called Thought Leader which helps prepare you for the process of landing and giving a TEDx talk. In the process of applying for TEDx talks, I learned that on average it took seventy-seven applications before an applicant landed a talk. It was helpful to know this because to me it sounded like a numbers game. I didn't take the failures personally. I focused more on the progress of applying to as many events as I could than the rejection rate. Call me lazy, but I applied to sixty events and called it a day.

I didn't take the failures personally.

The second to last event I applied for and the only application that was accepted was at The University of Purdue. Life is a numbers game, so let's aim for progress and not take failure so personally. We will never be perfect. That is okay! Even just writing that down gives me so much relief. We don't need to try and be something we are not. It doesn't mean we don't need to shoot for big goals or have any aspirations. What it means is, when we fail at reaching our goals, we can still appreciate the big picture.

When we come across the hills of West Virginia, we can walk it out. Even if it's at a slow pace, Confucius says we just need to keep moving. If we know it may take years to reach our dreams, we can choose to be patient and embrace the journey of progress like Jonathan Roumie. We can receive fifty-nine rejections and let it not phase us. The masterpiece of our dream is there. We just need to step back from the painting.

CHOOSE PROGRESS OVER PERFECTION

Brady shrugging off Day 193 in Arizona

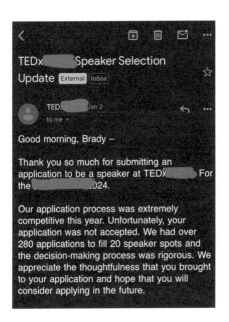

One of the many rejection emails Brady received

while applying to be a TEDx speaker

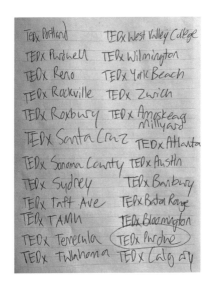

The backside list to Brady's sixty TEDx applications

EXERCISE:

Are you a perfectionist?

_____

_____

_____

_____

_____

Do you let perfectionism get in the way of your own progress?

_____

_____

_____

_____

_____

What is one way you can choose progress over perfection in your life?

_____

_____

_____

_____

_____

CHAPTER 13

LAST CHANCE, ALL IN!

In 2005, David Choe, was offered 60,000 dollars or stock options to paint a startup's headquarters in Palo Alto, California. Choe believed in the founder and thought, "this kid knows something and I'm going to bet my money on him". While Choe needed the money at the time, he opted out on the guaranteed money and took the stock options - he went all in. Seven years later, Choe's stock options in that startup, Facebook, were worth over 200 million dollars [24].

I will always remember one distinct phrase my professor William Neumann used during my undergraduate studies at The University of Arizona. The class had hundreds of students, and in order to take attendance in an efficient manner, we were each given clickers. We were given something like thirty seconds to click in when the class started, and as time winded down Professor Neumann always said the phrase, "Last chance, all in!" He said it every class! If you didn't click in on time, you were marked absent. It was a strict rule, but it represented a concept that I think is crucial when following a dream. You are either all in on your dream or you are not. But, you can't be in-between. You either get full credit or zero credit. You either will do whatever it takes to bring your dream to life, or you are not.

Multi Golden Globe and Academy Award winning actor, Denzel Washington, once said, "If I am going to fall, I don't want to fall back on anything except my faith. I want to fall forward, I figure at least this way I'll see what I'm going to hit" [25]. Backup plans can quickly become subtle excuses to stop chasing your dreams. If you have no plan B when times get hard, you will stay in the ring.

You are either all in on your dream or you are not.

You will keep fighting for your dream. This idea of charging towards the unknown without a back up plan is not new. In fact, in wartime people often referred to this concept as, "Burning The Ships!"

On February 18, 1519, Hernan Cortes led his men towards a city called Tenochtitlan, 200 miles away from Cuba. Just before the expedition, the governor of Cuba sent orders to Cortes to relieve him of his command. Cortes defied the governor and sailed towards Tenochtitlan in hopes to conquer land and gold. Cortes knew if he ever returned to Cuba he would face imprisonment or death.

There was only one way forward. Some of Cortes' men remained loyal to the governor of Cuba and tried to escape back to Cuba by boat. Cortes burned their boats and every boat sank. Whether his men liked it or not, they would either conquer land with Cortes or die. Retreating was no longer an option for his men. Cortes and his men were successful in conquering and settling the land they tried to seize [26]. I am not suggesting that you seize land or disobey a Governor's orders, but you can go all in on your dream.

We planned to depart for the cross country run on May 5, 2019. The RV company we rented from told us our camper would be ready for pick up on Saturday, May 4. We were in business to start on May 5. I called the RV company on Saturday morning and they told me that the RV wouldn't be ready for pickup until Monday, May 6. When we heard this news, Nate and I were in an Uber with all our suitcases from New York to New Jersey. I told the RV company we needed the RV that day, or else it would be a dealbreaker for us. The RV company found a way to expedite their cleaning process and we picked up our RV that morning just as we planned. I like to believe this "all in" approach was the reason behind finding an RV in time for our expedition. I put my life on hold and invested a lot of money into the run across America. In any investment, you can lose money. I was aware that paying my crewmate and renting an RV could all be for nothing if I didn't successfully achieve my dream. If the journey across America ended early, not only would I have been shattered, but my bank account would have been too. These were all risks that I knew very well but accepted.

Over the last ten years, there were many times I risked my time, finances, lifestyle, mental and physical health, and so much more to go all in on my dreams. I could have failed miserably running across America. I could have failed miserably starting a clothing company. I could have failed miserably with my recent TEDx talk. I hope I don't fail miserably with this book! Success is not guaranteed when you go all in on your dreams. That is okay! Why? Because nothing in life is guaranteed. Super Bowl MVP Champion Ray Lewis says, "Effort? Nobody can judge that. Because effort is between you and you." The only thing we can control is how much effort we put towards our dream. Only you know if you burned the ships and left everything out on the field.

In every dream I have chased, I have known that I have to take the shot. Even if I miss, I can have peace knowing I tried. Hockey legend Wayne Gretzky once famously said, "You miss 100% of the shots you don't take." I can confidently say that I have so much peace from going all in on my dreams. I sleep easy at night knowing I give all of myself and nothing less towards my dreams. I understand that at any moment of following my dreams, everything can crumble down in an instant. That is the risk of following a dream - a risk I am willing to take.

Is it time for you to go all in on a startup you believe in like Mr. Choe? Or, will retreating be an option for you like Cortes? Do you want to fall back towards your dreams or fall forward like Denzel Washington? Whatever you choose to do, promise me that you will leave it all out on the field. This is full credit or nothing. Only you and God know whether you clicked in or not.

Even if I miss, I can have peace knowing I tried.

If you are still with me and have read this far, chances are that some of these stories have struck a chord with you. Unless you skipped right to this Chapter, your dream has been circulating in your mind for a while now. Good! Although I enjoy storytelling, that is not the point of this book. The point of this book is for you to take your shot. I can't take the shot for you.

Sunny Co Clothing wouldn't exist if I didn't tell my roommate the idea on the way back from the football game. My run across America really wouldn't have occurred if I didn't show up to that run club. My TEDx talk wouldn't have happened if I didn't reach out to Jake for more information.

Will you fail miserably like I have many times in my life? Maybe. But what if you don't? What if you are just one step away from changing your life? You just need to take one step. *It all starts with one step.*

LAST CHANCE, ALL IN!

Brady delivering his first TEDx talk at The University of Purdue

Brady running into the Pacific Ocean after 218 days of running across USA

EXERCISE:

Are you all in on your dream right now?

_____

_____

_____

_____

_____

_____

If not, why? What is holding you back?

_____

_____

_____

_____

_____

If you have made it this far in the book, perhaps it is because you have a dream that is ready to be born.

GO

FOR

IT.

Postface

I truly believe that we all have wonderful gifts to share with the world, we just need to take one step towards them. My goal is that you find the courage to take a step towards your dreams after reading this book. If you so boldly take that step, a whole world of possibilities stands on the other side. I poured my heart and soul into these words. I do not take it lightly that you just spent valuable time out of your life to read this book. Thank you so very much! **Finally, one of my dreams is to make this book my first ever bestseller**. Why? Because if this book changes one person's life, I believe it could change many more. As I said in Chapter 9, I can't do this all on my own. I need your help. You can help me! Here are some easy and quick things you can do to help this book become a bestseller: Skydive with the book, swim with sharks and the book, do the splits while reading the book, backflip with the book, surf a giant wave with the book, ski a mountain with the book, run a marathon with the book, break dance with the book. I am completely kidding about all of those things. Believe it or not, if you really want to help this book sell around the world, there is a simple formula. If you do one of these three things below, I bet we could make this a bestseller! (bonus credit if you do all three!)

-Tell a friend about it (old school)

-Leave a review on Amazon or online (#FIRE)

-Gift it to someone (sharing is caring)

Speaking

Thanks to social media, Brady has inspired millions of people from all across the world with his inspiring message. While he no longer is on social media, Brady speaks across the country at private events and reminds others that anything is possible. His message resonates with all types of people. If you or someone you know would like to book Brady to speak at your next event, whether it be for business, sports, philanthropy, personal, or anything else, please reach out to our team at the email provided below.

speaking@bradysilverwood.com

Connect with Brady

While Brady is no longer on Instagram and Tik Tok, he does keep up with his Youtube Channel. If you leave a comment on one of his videos, he will try his best to respond. If you enjoyed this book and left a review online, shared the book with a friend, or told someone about the book, he would like to thank you personally!

Brady Silverwood- Ultra Runner, Author, Speaker
Scan QR code below for Brady's YouTube Channel

Acknowledgments:

This page could be a whole book in itself but I will do my best to keep it brief.

I first off want to thank God for everything I have been blessed with in this life. God, you have been by my side always throughout this journey. Everything has been made possible through your grace.

Mom and Dad - you have also been by my side every step of this journey and you are the best parents in the world.

Carly, Cristie, Katelyn, Jimmy, and Adam - I love you all so much and feel so lucky to call you all family. My four nephews Caleb, Henry, Owen, and Austin - I love you more than you know and you are all the real reason I come to visit family! Thank you to the rest of my family and friends for always supporting me and being there for me.

Special thanks to Luke Gledhill for your leadership and guidance over the years, I really don't know if any of this would have happened if you didn't harass me over text about that darn run club.

I couldn't have published this book without the exceptional support from my editor, Danyel Meahan. You are the flow master Danyel! Your editing helped bring so much more clarity and vibrance to the words in this book. Thank you for giving me support when I was feeling imposter syndrome during the editing process.

I need to also thank Kyle Aitken! Kyle, thank you for creating a masterpiece cover design for this book. I am the least artistic person and you exceeded my expectations for what I envisioned.

You never know the difference you make in someone's life, as small as it may seem. Which brings me to my last acknowledgement: The baristas Syn & Cailey at Huriyali and Tyler & Alicia at Second State Coffee, thank you for serving me the best coffee every day - saying hi to y'all everyday I came in to work on this book was a blessing!

Notes

1.   Montag, Ali. "Billionaire Alibaba Founder Jack Ma Was Rejected from Every Job He Applied to after College, even KFC." CNBC. August 10, 2017. https://www.cnbc.com/2017/08/09/lesson-alibabas-jack-ma-learned-after-being-rejected-for-a-job-at-kfc.html.

2.   Weinraub, Bernard. "A Comic on the Edge at $7 Million a Movie." *The New York Times*, August 1, 1994. https://www.nytimes.com/1994/08/01/movies/a-comic-on-the-edge-at-7-million-a-movie.html.

3.   Hamdy, Sam. "From Rejection to Recognition: The Inspiring Story of J.K. Rowling." Medium. January 27, 2023. https://thesamhamdy.medium.com/from-rejection-to-recognition-the-inspiring-story-of-j-k-rowling-117b2f093860.

4.   Dwyre, Bill. "Zenyatta Is 20 Years Old. Her Legend in Horse Racing Still Shines Bright." *Los Angeles Times*, December 31, 2023. https://www.latimes.com/sports/story/2023-12-31/zenyatta-is-20-years-old-horse-racing-legend-still-shines.

5.   Dwyre, Bill. "Perfection Eludes Zenyatta in a Breeders' Cup Classic Loss." *Los Angeles Times*, November 7, 2010. https://

www.latimes.com/archives/la-xpm-2010-nov-07-la-sp-dwyre-breeders-cup-20101107-story.html.

6.   "Lobster Institute." The University of Maine. Accessed March 7, 2024. https://umaine.edu/lobsterinstitute/educational-resources/life-cycle-reproduction/.

7.   "David Goggins' Incredible Life Story Will Motivate and Inspire You - Pickler & Ben." Pickler and Ben. March 15, 2019. Video, https://www.youtube.com/watch?v=rH94RYeeTeA.

8.   Lewis Howes, "877 Navy Seal Mindset for Living Your Best Life with Chadd Wright," November, 2019 in *School of Greatness*, produced by Greatness Media, podcast, https://open.spotify.com/episode/4uhY4ah9zLsiCwFVUqEbG5?si=9zpVFEIOQpCxzsbk-0APXg&nd=1&dlsi=80a41a24dd314074.

9.   "I Washed All Of The Dishes | Jesse Itzler." Jesseitzler4. Video, https://www.youtube.com/shorts/_zxjrnMSMco?app=desktop.

10.   Colin O' Brady. January 9, 2023. Video, https://www.instagram.com/colinobrady/reel/Cnm13SKoIT2/.

11.   "How to 'overcome' Fear | Trevor Ragan | TEDxCedarRapids." TEDx Talks. June 14, 2018. Video, https://www.youtube.com/watch?v=xrWvPo-KaVs.

12.   Sinek, Simon. 2017. *Leaders Eat Last.* 1st ed. Penguin Publishing Group.

13.   "Desmond Doss: The Real Story." Desmond Doss. Accessed March 5, 2024. https://desmonddoss.com/bio/bio-real.php.

14.   Kenney, Kirk. "Tiger Woods' 2008 U.S. Open Victory at Torrey Pines 'Probably the Best Ever'." *The San Diego Union-Tribune*, June 13, 2021.

15.   *Tiger*. HBO Sports, Jigsaw Productions, Our Time Projects, 2021.

16.   "Top NBA Finals Moments: Michael Jordan's Flu Game in 1997 Finals." NBA. September 14, 2021. https://www.nba.com/news/history-finals-moments-jordan-flu-game-1997.

17.   "'That Was a Cool Feeling': An Oral History of Kirk Gibson's Iconic 1988 Home Run." SI. October 13, 2015. https://www.si.com/mlb/2013/10/15/kirk-gibson-dennis-eckersley-dodgers-athletics-1988-world-series-home-run-oral-history.

18.   "Famous Quotes by Thomas Edison." Thomas Alva Edison Foundations. Accessed March 10, 2024. https://www.thomasedison.org/edison-quotes.

19.   Waksman, Gary, director. *Four Days in October*. ESPN, MLB, 2010.

20.   "What Oprah Learned from Jim Carrey | Oprah's Life Class | Oprah Winfrey Network." OWN. October 13, 2011. Video, https://www.youtube.com/watch?v=nPU5bjzLZX0.

21.   "Crazy Faith // Crazy Faith (Part 1)." Transformation Church. August 12, 2019. Video, https://www.youtube.com/watch?v=uiR8TLiyfnc&t=3687s

22.   "Vision Board The Secret John Assaraf Larry King OneCoach." VisionBoard. February 8, 2007. Video, https://www.youtube.com/watch?v=kVVOQVgvaWU.

23.   Stewart, Daniel, director. *Chosen Docuseries: Jonathan And Jesus.* Lionsgate Entertainment, Inc., 2024.

24.   England, Lucy. "The Artist Who Painted Facebook's 1st Office Took Stock Instead of Cash — And now He Is Worth $200 Million." Business Insider. June 9, 2015.

25.   "Denzel Washington - University of Pennsylvania." Vidbi. June 14, 2016. Video, https://www.youtube.com/watch?v=JEFbfwg9dek&t=487s.

26.   "Cortés Burns His Boats." PBS. Accessed March 4, 2024. https://www.pbs.org/conquistadors/cortes/cortes_d00.html.

" I can do all things through Christ which strengtheneth me"

(Philippians 4:13; KJV)

Made in the USA
Columbia, SC
16 April 2024

34455697R00080